BIBLICAL AND POST-BIBLICAL DEFILEMENT AND MOURNING: LAW AS THEOLOGY

THE LIBRARY OF JEWISH LAW AND ETHICS

Edited by Norman Lamm

Jakob and Erna Michael professor of Jewish philosophy
Yeshiva University

BIBLICAL AND POST-BIBLICAL DEFILEMENT AND MOURNING: LAW AS THEOLOGY

By

EMANUEL FELDMAN

YESHIVA UNIVERSITY PRESS
KTAV PUBLISHING HOUSE, INC.
NEW YORK
1977

Library of Congress Cataloging in Publication Data
Feldman, Emanuel, 1927—
  Biblical and post-Biblical defilement and mourning.
  (The Library of Jewish law and ethics)
  Bibliography: p.
  Includes indexes.
  1. Death (Judaism) 2. Death—Biblical teaching.
3. Purity, Ritual (Judaism) 4. Purity, Ritual—Biblical
teaching. 5. Mourning (Jewish law)
I. Title.
BM635.4.F44   296.3′3   76-41187
ISBN 0-87068-287-3

MANUFACTURED IN THE UNITED STATES OF AMERICA

CONTENTS

SECTION I

DEATH AND DEFILEMENT IN THE
ANCIENT WORLD AND IN THE BIBLE

CHAPTER I

CHAPTER II

CHAPTER III

CHAPTER IV

SECTION II

DEATH AND MOURNING: ESTRANGEMENT
AND DESACRALIZATION IN PRACTICE

CHAPTER I

CHAPTER II

CHAPTER III

Acknowledgments

Thanks are due to the following for permission to reproduce material by this author which first appeared in their pages.
The Jewish Quarterly Review, Volume LXIII, 1972-1973.
Judaism, Volume 21, No. 1, Winter, 1972.
Jewish Reflections on Death, ed. Jack Riemer, Schocken Books, 1974.

Abbreviations

AZ—'Abodah Zarah

BB—Baba Bathra

Bekh.—Bekhoroth

Ber.—Berakhoth

BQ—Baba Qamma

BM—Baba Mezi'a

Er.—'Erubin

Keth.—Kethuboth

Qidd.—Qiddushin

Meg.—Megillah

Men.—Menahoth

MQ—Mo'ed Qatan

Ned.—Nedarim

Nid.—Niddah

RH—Rosh Hashanah

Sanh.—Sanhedrin

Shabb.—Shabbath

Tem.—Temurah

Yad.—Yadayim

Yeb.—Yebamoth

Zeb.—Zebahim

J. prefixed to the name of tractate indicates a reference to the Jerusalemite (Palestinian) Talmud. MR refers to the Midrash Rabbah Gen. R., Ex. R., etc., refer to the Midrash Rabbah on that particular book. Unless another edition is specified, the Midrash Rabbah utilized here is the Vilna, 1911 edition.[1]

Abbreviations Used for Books and Journals Cited

ANET—*Ancient Near Eastern Texts,* by J. B. Pritchard (Princeton, 1950).

BA—*The Biblical Archaeologist*

BDB—Brown, Driver, and Briggs, *A Hebrew and English Lexicon of the Old Testament* (Boston, 1907).

BASOR—*Bulletin of the American Schools of Oriental Research*

BJRL—*Bulletin of the John Rylands Library*

HTR—*Harvard Theological Review*

HUCA—*Hebrew Union College Annual*

IEJ—*Israel Exploration Journal*

JQR—*Jewish Quarterly Review*

JAOS—*Journal of the American Oriental Society*
JBR—*Journal of Bible and Religion*
JBL—*Journal of Biblical Literature*
JNES—*Journal of Near Eastern Studies*
JJS—*Journal of Jewish Studies*
JSS—*Journal of Semitic Studies*
PEQ—*Palestine Exploration Quarterly*
VT—*Vetus Testamentum*
ZAW—*Zeitschrift für die alttestamentliche Wissenschaft*

1. The entire Babylonian Talmud is available in English translation in the London, 1948, edition published by Soncino Press. Soncino has also published an English translation of Midrash Rabbah (1939). References to the law code of Maimonides, which is known as *Mishneh Torah*, are available in English in the Yale Judaica Series.

Editor's Foreword

The Angel of Death has, in our days, "come out of the closet." It was not too long ago that death was ignored in the magical hope that it would go away if its name was not invoked. It was not mentioned in polite company; was rarely analyzed even by scholars, psychologists, and physicians; and, so great the terror that it struck in the hearts of the most sophisticated and the apparently most self-confident, that a thriving industry developed in America in disguising it when, ubiquitous as it is, it inevitably came.

But death, like life, has its changing fortunes. This most universal and inexorable of events was "exposed" and forced into popular consciousness and into the public forum in a series of popular works. Jessica Mitford, Eliza Kübler-Ross, and Ernest Becker, amongst others, have made death "respectable." Their works, each in a different way, have made it possible to discuss the phenomenon of death rationally and humanly.

Yet such is the pendulum of fashion, that "thanatology" seems ready to be undone by success. Death, in a manner of speaking, is being talked to death. It has become popular on campuses and in discussion groups throughout the land. It is so much an "in thing," that many a naive person believes that it is our generation that discovered death, and that the ancients had little of value to say about it. This transcendental ignorance of the wealth of material and insights in ancient cultures on the subject is often so pervasive as to lend a note of unreality, and certainly parochialism, to too much of the contemporary discourse on the theme.

Scholars have, of course, been aware of the long history of human contemplation of death in various cultures. The taboos, the magic, the ritual, the mythology—all have been recorded, if not studied in sufficient depth.

Of all the views of death, that of the Jewish tradition has probably been least examined and even less understood and appreciated. Partly, this may be the consequence of the facile assumption that Judaism is merely part of the rest of the ancient civilizations, with their irrational superstitions, and hence with no enlightenment to yield for modern man. Partly, too, it may be because so much of the Jewish tradition is formulated in halakhic terms, and Jewish law is simply too arcane and too esoteric for the anthropologist or historian who is not an expert in Judaism's highly developed and sophisticated legal code.

Of late, however, this situation is being rectified. A few years ago, Rabbi Maurice Lamm's volume on *The Jewish Way in Death and Mourning* presented the Halakhah of mourning with a clarity and simplicity that made it a popular manual for families that suffered bereavement and now had available, in lucid English, a guide to authentic Jewish conduct.

The current volume by Dr. Emanuel Feldman adds new dimensions to this articulation of the Jewish tradition on death and mourning. Rabbi Feldman combines many disciplines in this knowledgeable and scholarly opus. History, anthropology, Biblical scholarship, psychology, halakhic expertise—all are brought together and focused on a theme that runs through the entire tradition. Here is a work of scholarship that avoids the clichés and facile pronouncements of the faddists. It speaks in the measured voice of the careful academician—and yet illuminates the subject, allowing us to view a great theme without obscurantism or pedantry. It is, therefore, a welcome addition to the Library of Jewish Law and Ethics.

In a word, Dr. Feldman's present work breathes new life into the subject of death from the Jewish point of view.

NORMAN LAMM

August 17, 1976

Introduction

The post-biblical legal system, formulated in Midrash, Mishnah, and Talmud—and known as *halakhah,* "the way"—is, on the surface, nothing more than a collection of arcane minutiae covering every conceivable daily act of a human being. Like any legal system, it gives no rationale for the behavior it prescribes.

It is the underlying assumption of this study that this legal system is more than a dry compendium of directives for daily life and that contained within it are specific patterns of belief, thought, and attitude; in brief, that the *halakhah* contains within it an implicit theology.

These are the areas chosen for examination in this study:
1. *tum'ah*/defilement,[1] especially defilement resulting from death;
2. the laws of mourning, as they illustrate the "theology of defilement";
3. the rabbinic funeral lament.

These subjects reveal significant insights into the biblical/rabbinic ideas of man's relationship to God, to life, to death, and to himself.

A study of this type is beset by a number of difficulties. While numerous "Old Testament theologies" are available, studies of rabbinic or halakhic theology are very rare. Even in the biblical theologies, modern scholars have by and large ignored the rabbinic view of the Bible. The result is that the study of post-biblical theology—and, especially, the theology of post-biblical law—has been cast into virtual oblivion.

The problem is compounded by the fact that Judaism is an actional rather than a speculative creed. Its religious literature primarily reflects the practical duties of daily life rather than flights of philosophic and theological speculation.

Rabbinic literature, for example, makes it quite clear that the precepts of the Bible require no rational basis. Two biblical commandments—the restrictions placed on an Israelite king regarding the multiplying of horses and of wives (Deuteronomy 17:16-17)—were recorded with their reasons, and because of this, "the greatest in the world [Solomon] was caused to stumble." Therefore, says Sanhedrin 21b, no rationale is given for commandments. The great rationalist of Jewish thought, Maimonides, characteristically records no reasons for the various precepts in his monumental *Mishneh Torah,* which is the authoritative post-biblical sourcebook of Jewish law. For believers, reasons are not necessary; for non-believers, reasons are of no avail.

This is not to say that Judaism's legal system has not been subjected to repeated attempts at establishing some overarching rationale. A belief in the divinity of the laws has as its corollary a belief that the *halakhah,* while surely transcending human categories of thought, is a muffled echo of the divine will. Thus, Philo among the Hellenists, Judah Ha-Levi, Ibn Ezra, Maimonides, Nahmanides, and Albo of the Middle Ages; and David Hoffman and Samson Raphael Hirsch in modern times, are but a few of the powerful forces in the thrust of the literature of *taamei ha-mitzvot,* "reasons for the commandments." [2]

The motives of these philosophers are varied. We find apologetics as well as attempts to strengthen observance among the Jews; defense of Judaism from non-Jewish attacks, and efforts to justify the ways of God to man; speculations about the social, hygienic, moral, psychological, ethical, and utilitarian benefits of the commandments, as well as their role in helping man attain wisdom, perfection and eternal life.

There has thus been no dearth of rationalistic approaches to the commandments of Judaism as a whole. What has been lacking is a systematic and thorough investigation, in theological terms, of a single type of biblical commandment and its post-biblical exegesis and application.

This is particularly true in areas such as "defilement," which are the classic prototypes of *huqim*—"statutes"—for which there are no readily understood reasons and which are to be accepted on faith.

The *tum'ah* legislation in the Bible and in post-biblical literature is staggering in its complexity. Even Solomon, the wisest of men, is described as having said of the purification rites for a man defiled by the dead, "I said, I will get wisdom, but it was far from me." [3] In fact, the Talmudic Order dealing with *tum'ah* is called *da'at*, "Knowledge," by the Talmud itself. [4] And the Rabbis indicate how learned the people once were by pointing out that in the times of Hezekiah, everyone from Dan to Beersheba was examined and found to be an expert in the laws of *tum'ah*. [5]

The rabbinic legislation on defilement constitutes most of the order of *Toharot* ("Pure Things"), and its study is considered most difficult. A thorough knowledge of *tum'ah* was one of the prerequisites for sitting on the Sanhedrin. [6] The teacher Symmachus is praised because he knew forty-eight reasons for every aspect of *tum'ah* and its purification. [7] The children in the times of King David were praiseworthy because they were able to understand the laws of defilement and purity in all their complexities. [8]

One is particularly sobered by the incident told of R. Johanan b. Zakkai. An idolator once questioned him about the ritual of the Red Heifer, which purifies from death defilement, although the one in charge of the purification process himself becomes defiled. [9] R. Johanan replied that the process is designed to make the impure spirit flee. The text continues:

> When the idolator departed, the disciples said, This heathen have you fended off with a reed, but what will you say to us? He said to them, By your lives, the dead does not defile nor does the water purify, it is rather the decree of the King, the Holy One blessed be He, who has said, I have established a statute, I have decreed a decree, and you are not permitted to violate them, as it is written (Numbers 19:2): "This is the statute of the Torah which the Lord has commanded." [10]

Maimonides in his *Mishneh Torah* echoes this sentiment in the introduction to Toharot. This subject, he writes, "bristles with difficulties far from human understanding, and is one which even the great Sages of the Mishnah found hard to comprehend." In this same work, in his chapter, "Immersion Pools" (11:12), he states that these laws are Scriptural decrees "and not matters about which human understanding is capable of forming judgment." (Maimonides does, however, offer a symbolic interpretation of defilement in this very chapter.) And, in a striking image, the Midrash notes that the Holy One Himself was once discovered by Moses to be deeply engrossed in studying the laws of the Red Heifer.[11]

It is, perhaps, because of its very complexity that the research into defilement has been so limited. An examination of the literature, other than primary material, reminds one that little has changed since R. Eliezer's prophetic plaint two millennia ago:

> I have studied three hundred laws on the subject of a deep bright spot (a form of leprosy defilement: Leviticus 12:2), yet no man has ever asked me about them.[12]

In truth, very few scholars have "asked about them" or have been concerned with a "theology of defilement." In modern times, Samson Raphael Hirsch makes a brief study of *tum'ah* in his *Horeb,*[13] while David Hoffmann touches on it in his commentary on Leviticus.[14] There have been systematic attempts to find a philosophy of *halakhah*,[15] but an investigation of a consistent life view that may be found in the specific *tum'ah* legislation is not available.

In view of all this, it would be presumptuous to claim that the present study of defilement will offer a definitive rationale and understanding of such a complex subject. What it does propose to do, however, is to make an exploratory investigation: to reconnoiter the territory and determine if any consistent patterns of thought are discernible. It is our working hypothesis that the *tum'ah* legislation is fertile ground for such exploration, and that within it can be perceived the outlines of the Israelite interpretation of existence. This interpretation, it will be seen, is unusually consistent in rabbinic literature, despite the span of several centuries and of various types of literature—legal, homiletic, mystical—which it encompasses.

We will undertake this exploration, first, by establishing Israel's view of death within the context of ancient civilization. This will lead to a survey of Israel's *tum'ah* legislation, and to a discussion of a recurring and fundamental point of our thesis: Death is the utmost desacralization and, in the biblical/rabbinic scheme, defilement represents estrangement from the Divine. We will support this idea by attempting to show how God is synonymous with life, and how absence of life—as seen from within the *tum'ah* legislation—is a key element in defilement.

The second major section will investigate the post-biblical mourning legislation—centered primarily on Talmudic literature—and will show how the detailed regimen of mourning symbolizes the estrangement of the mourner from God, from his community, and from himself.

The aspects of estrangement resulting from defilement are further underscored by certain rabbinic parallels between the laws of the mourner and those of the excommunicant, and by the rabbinic concept of *lo'eg larash,* "mocking the dead."

In connection with mourning, we will present a detailed analysis of the Rabbinic Lament, which, in its profane characteristics, is a literary manifestation of desacralization and cultic estrangement.

I hereby express my gratitude to my father, Rabbi Joseph H. Feldman, of Jerusalem, Israel, for reading parts of the manuscript and for pointing out various relevant source materials for this study; to my brother, Rabbi Aaron Feldman, of Jerusalem, Israel, who read the entire draft and made many important corrections and helpful suggestions; and to Prof. Frederick C. Prussner and Prof. Martin J. Buss of Emory University, who were generous with their time, encouragement, and skillful counsel. It goes without saying that the errors and imperfections in this book —as well as the responsibility for any conclusions—are solely mine, and not theirs in any way.

Emanuel Feldman
Atlanta, Georgia
Ab, 5736
August, 1976

SECTION I

DEATH AND DEFILEMENT IN THE ANCIENT WORLD AND IN THE BIBLE

Chapter One

Primitive Man and Death: Representative Views

The concept of the dead as a force of impurity and defilement pervades the entire life view of primitive man, with echoes that resound in prehistory. In primitive man's world, the dead are taboo and are completely avoided. The earlier anthropologists almost unanimously attributed these taboos to fear of the dead. To Frazer, for example, fear of the dead is one of the powerful forces in primitive religion. He points out that special costumes worn by mourners were originally intended to be disguises. Bright colors were predominant, and the mourners would paint their own bodies with bright red or white, primarily in order to ward off the possible return of the spirits. This fear also expressed itself in certain elements of hygiene and reflected the concern with disease and contamination.[1]

In primitive religions, the departed spirits not only exist, but exert a strong influence on the living because of their supposed extensive powers. The living are forced always to be on guard against them, and it is fear rather than affection which dominates the attitude of the living toward the dead. There are, for example, ingenious and resourceful attempts to bar the house against unwelcome intrusions by these spirits. Primitive man instinctively

3

feels that they constantly hover over him and that they may be ready to take him away with them to an unknown world.[2] He tries to rid himself of these dangerous forces either by persuasion and conciliation, or by force and fraud. He erects barriers of fire or other physical barriers against their return, or he ties up, mutilates, or maims the dead bodies. He may even destroy the property the dead have left behind, thus offering them no reason to return to claim or enjoy anything.

Lods is typical of the biblical scholars who have been influenced by this anthropological orthodoxy. He takes the classic practices and taboos of the mourners and finds in them the dominant theme of fear. The sackcloth is apotropaeic, in that it makes the living unrecognizable to the feared spirits or ghosts that may be returning. The covering or veiling of the mourner's head has a similar purpose. He sees in the entire range of mourning rites an attempt to keep the living from any contact with the dreaded and all-powerful underworld.[3]

For Lods, the varying beliefs and feelings about death can be tied into a neat evolutionary package. First, a fearful power was attributed to the dead. Then, under the influence of Israelite religion, the dead were considered permanently banished to *Sheol,* the netherworld from which there could be no return. Only later, according to this typically Hegelian view of religion, were the two ideas reconciled and placed side by side.

Oesterley finds that a number of mourning practices are protective measures against hostile acts which may be forthcoming from the spirits.[4] Elhorst and Sheftelowitz see in funerary rites an expression of this fear and a desire to placate.[5] And Edwin O. James suggests that the primitive habit of burying a body in a flexed position may have been a kind of precaution against the possibility of the dead person's "walking" and wreaking vengeance upon the living.[6]

The theory of fear, then, is for some investigators the touchstone of the universal taboo surrounding the dead and the root element in the ritual defilement or contamination resulting from contact with the dead. And the Levitical purity laws concerning *tum'ah,* it is maintained, are but the logical corollary of these fear-generated taboos. Ringgren is typical of this school when he writes that the biblical legislation concerning the defilement of the dead is merely a codification of the "natural reaction to the unknown and sinister." [7]

Louis Finkelstein has an even more mundane view of the defilement taboos: "In a semi-tropical climate a human corpse is one of the foremost sources of disease, and those touching it are rightly separated from the community for a time." According to him, the *tum'ah* laws might once have been ceremonial rites, but with the advent of festival worship at the Temple and the ensuing press of huge crowds, the Levitical laws "were rules of health which alone prevented each festival from leading to an epidemic." The defilement precautions, he writes, were essentially hygienic, necessary "to the welfare of Jerusalem's many thousands." [8]

Finkelstein's thesis overlooks several essential features of the defilement legislation. First, defilement restrictions apply not only to public festival rites and crowded cities but to private and individual contexts as well, such as the eating of the *terumah* (heave offering) by the individual priest outside the confines of the Temple.[9]

Second, and even more important, is the fact that the interdiction against sacrificing while in a state of defilement is overridden in the case of an "offering which has a fixed time." All congregational—and public—offerings have fixed times. When the time of that offering arrives, and it happens that the majority of the congregation bringing the offering is defiled by a corpse, the offering is not postponed; it is brought while the congregation is in a state of defilement.[10] In fact, it is exclusively corpse defilement which is overridden, and not defilement of emissions, creeping things, carrion, and the like. "Corpse uncleanness alone was allowed to be set aside."[11] If the defilement laws were merely hygienic precautions, it is difficult to explain how it was that precisely at crowded festivals—at which congregational offerings were brought—those very corpse-defilement laws were set aside in order not to postpone an offering.

Otto plays a variation, albeit a more sophisticated one, on the theme of fear.[12] The unclean was originally that which was loathsome. The dead exercised a spell on the living only because they were considered things of horror through the feeling of disgust at their "revoltingness"—or because man's own will to live was disturbed. But this is not a natural folk feeling; it had to be learned from others. For Otto, the original perception about uncleanness developed and passed over into the sphere of the numinous and then achieved numinous horror, whether or not the dead aroused natural disgust. The original horror of the dead, natural or not, was transformed into terror before the sacred power of the dead. The sacred is numinous, an aspect of divine power, and as Eliade interprets Otto, death signifies a passing from the status of the profane to that of the sacred.[13]

Eichrodt also places great stress on the idea of fear as the basis for the taboo surrounding death. The ancient Israelite customs of mourning—rending garments, wearing sackcloth, scattering ashes—have their origin in "an attempt to make one's self unrecognizable to the dead for fear of their envy or malice."[14] For example, the Sumatrans make loud noises at their interment ceremonies, and remove the body not through the regular door but through a hole broken in the wall of the hut. They want to make certain that the spirit does not find its way back to the living. Similarly, according to Eichrodt, the defilement legislation in Numbers 19:15—"Every open vessel on which there is not a closely fitting cover is unclean"—is a manifestation of the fear that the "spirit of the dead may try to hide itself in the house in order to avoid having to enter the grave with the corpse." [15]

Anthropologists since Frazer have also stressed this element of fear among the primitives. Levy-Bruhl observes that among the New Guinea tribesmen, "the belief is held that the dead do not really depart until certain ceremonies are fulfilled, and that they need to be pacified and cajoled" because they are hostile and jealous of the living.[16] Elsewhere, Levy-Bruhl suggests that the concern of the primitives is whether or not the deceased has definitely left this world.[17] Elkin's study of Australian aborigines corroborates this observation. Mourning customs, he indicates, are faithfully observed so that the deceased will not be angry with his group.[18]

Although most of the early anthropologists took it for granted that the fear of the dead is instinctive—and even suggested that this is an important factor in much of religious thought [19]—the idea of instinctive fear is refuted by more recent scolarship. Radcliffe-Brown, discussing the Andaman tribesmen's burial customs, denies any such natural fear and points rather to a combination of a learned fear and affection.[20] Sylvia Anthony maintains that children's reactions to death are largely devoid of anxiety, that it is only at a later stage that this reaction changes, and that attitudes toward death are not instinctive but, evidently, are learned.[21]

Freud, too, disagrees with the theory of instinctive fear. Just as relations among the living are themselves ambivalent, so also is the attitude of the living toward the dead, which includes feelings of guilt and concealed hostility. This, he claims, is the prototype of the general ambivalence of human emotions, evidence for which is found in mourning customs as well as in the so-called ruthlessness of the ancestors. Referring to primitive man's attitude toward death as "extremely contradictory," he writes:

On the one hand, he [primitive man] took death seriously, recognized it as the termination of life and used it to that end; on the other hand, he also denied death, reduced it to nothingness. . . . The law of ambivalence of feeling . . . had assuredly a very much wider validity in primitive periods.[22]

Martin-Achard also stresses this ambivalence: "The dead are at once mourned and dreaded." The sight and idea of death provokes "complex and contradictory reactions." [23]

Hertz goes one step further. The horror before the dead cannot be explained physically alone. It is also of a social kind. Societies regard themselves as ongoing entities and are threatened by the death of any individual. "Society is stricken in the very principle of its life, in the faith it has in itself." [24]

In sum, more recent scholarship has avoided the presumptions of Frazer and his school who believe that there is a uniform human reaction to natural phenomena like death. On the contrary, as Eliade has written, "man's reactions to nature are often conditioned by his culture and hence, finally, by history." [25]

The View of Death in the Ancient Near East

Before examining death from the perspective of biblical and post-biblical attitudes, it is instructive to examine the ways in which Israel's cultural and geographic neighbors of the ancient world—Egypt, Mesopotamia, and Canaan—saw the matter.[26]

For the Egyptians, the issue was not horror or fear of the dead; rather, it was the very existence of death, the great enemy, which posed the fundamental problem. They never quite came to terms with it, strove mightily to overcome its reality, and were convinced that through magical techniques they could delay, if not reverse, the fact of death. [27] In fact, the mummification process had as its central purpose the revivification of the dead, and the central theme of the Egyptian mortuary ritual was the "resusci-

tation" of the dead in order to enable him to continue his existence in the afterlife. The Egyptian religion was basically static.
Nothing changes, and the only significant feature of life is its
changelessness. [28] Life goes on even after death, and thus, during
his lifetime, the Egyptian was very careful to arrange for his own
embalming and to provide for his physical needs in the netherworld. Even the dramatic changes brought about by death were
not really dramatic. Nothing was changed by death; for the
Egyptian it had no final or ultimate power since man was able to
circumvent it. Death was simply a transition to a new life which
may turn out to be happier than the life on this earth since the
great enemy, death, has now been conquered. [29]

This attempt of the ancient Egyptians to overcome death's
reality is evident from the fact that death is not mentioned in
legal contracts. [30] Further, the death event itself is apparently
never depicted in Egyptian art. [31] Osiris, though he is frequently
shown lying dead and being mourned by Isis and Nephthys, is
never shown as being struck down by Set. Similarly, in the
Egyptian *Book of the Dead* we find many post-death scenes, but
the actual death of the person is never shown.

In Mesopotamia, on the other hand, there is little concern
with death or the afterlife. The view here is pessimistic about the
possiblity of achieving a happy destiny after death. [32] We find no
vast tombs or pyramids as in Egypt, and no elaborate mortuary
equipment as in Canaan. [33] It is true that climatic conditions in
this region did not allow the kind of physical preservation which
was possible in the dry Egyptian sands, but Mesopotamians also
possessed an entirely different world view. They reacted to death
almost laconically, without any major speculation about the
theological problem it posed. They considered nothing permanent
or secure, and no values could be truly enduring. Furthermore,
unlike Egypt, no single god in the Mesopotamian pantheon was
truly omnipotent since all the gods had themselves been created.

Consequently, nothing was truly stable or reassuring. The gods were in their heavens, true, but they were capricious and unpredictable and nothing was really right with the world. [34] This uncertainty was extended to the realm of death. It was important to utilize the correct forms in order to protect against heavenly caprice, but death was final and there was no point in frantic attempts to overcome it. Neither the Sumerian Inanna's "Descent to the Nether World" nor its Akkadian parallel, "Descent of Ishtar to the Nether World," [35] displays any frenetic speculation about death's philosophic difficulties. The dead simply go down to the "Land of No Return," the house which "none leave who have entered it." The existence of death is accepted fatalistically; undue energies are not expended on explanations. After all, the gods had created man in order to have servants to build temples and offer sacrifices. [36] Once men became incapable of performing, there was no purpose for their existence, and the quest for immortality in the Gilgamesh Epic is hopeless:

> The life which thou seekest thou wilt not find,
> When the gods created man
> they alloted death to mankind
> Life they retained in their keeping. [37]

With Neti, the chief gate-keeper of the netherworld, the Sumerians recognize, as does Hamlet millennia later—and in almost the same words—that one is led to death "on the road whose traveler returns not."

The Canaanites differ somewhat from both the Mesopotamians and the Egyptians. Vocal and defiant, the Canaanite mythopoeic literature set up divine rivals to death and granted them vast powers and huge kingdoms. The vigorous mythology personifies death as a powerful figure who is often able to do battle with the deity himself. [38] The Canaanites also believed that the dead lived on and needed the living to sustain them with food and drink. A Gezer burial cave, in use from 4000 to 2000, reveals equipment for serving liquid to the departed. [39] The mourning and the sacrifices offered for Baal were designed to help invigorate him and bring about his resurrection. [40] And like the Egyptians and the Mesopotamians, expensive jewels and weapons formed part of the mortuary equipment. It is evident from finds at Ḥazor, Megiddo, Taanach, Lachish, and Bet She'an that the Canaanites practiced a bold cult of the dead as a physical corollary of their energetic mythology. [41]

This brief summary suggests that the response of the ancient world to death manifests itself in several forms: in an attempt to ignore it, in a physical effort to overcome it, and in a matter-of-fact acceptance of its finality.

Chapter Two

Israel's View of Death: Biblical and Rabbinic

How does Israel react to death? The *tum'ah* legislation—preoccupied as it is with matters of death—as well as the mourning legislation, offer valuable insights into the biblical/rabbinic attitude toward death and life.

One fact is apparent. Neither in the biblical nor rabbinic legislation on defilement does one find the element of horror or fear. This may seem surprising in view of Israel's rigorous anti-death legislation. In the Bible, for example, that which has died attains the status of defilement: "he who toucheth the dead body of any human person shall be defiled for seven days" (Numbers 19:11), which is the longest possible period of defilement. (Compare, also, these verses: Numbers 9:6; 19:16, 18; 31:19.) Not only animate beings, but things and objects may become defiled by death.

> And everything upon which any part of them, when they are dead, doth fall, shall be unclean; whether it be any vessel of food or raiment or skin or sack, every vessel wherewith any work can be done . . . shall be unclean until the evening . . . . (Leviticus 11:32).

13

Furthermore, that which is *tamé,* or defiled, because of death has the power to transfer its *tum'ah* to other beings or objects by contact. Numbers 19:22: "Whatsoever the unclean person may touch shall be unclean. . . ." Mishnah Oholot 1:2 states, "Vessels which have come into contact with the dead, or with other [defiled] vessels, are *tamé* a *tum'ah* of seven days." Mishnah Kelim 2:1 ff. describes in detail the various types of vessels that are susceptible to defilement. Any person who is inherently in a higher status of sanctity, such as a priest or a Nazarite, is subject to more severe restrictions concerning the defiling power of the dead (Leviticus 21:1-6; Numbers 6:1-10). The legislation affecting priests is particularly relentless when it comes to death, with severe laws concerning defilement by a corpse. A priest, for example, may be in the proximity of a corpse only if it is a close relative. The high priest is even enjoined this proximity, and is forbidden to display any signs of mourning. (Leviticus 21:1-12).

It is important, however, not to fall into the temptation of misinterpreting the nature of the biblical *tum'ah* legislation. While it is true, as Kaufman has said, that the priestly laws "raise especially high barriers" against death and against defilement by a corpse,[42] it need not follow that this legislation reflects a fear of the dead. At a matter of fact—and this is overlooked by almost all discussants of this theme—the severity of the anti-*tum'ah* legislation applies exclusively to the priest. *Neither in biblical nor rabbinic law is there a prohibition against a lay Israelite's or Nazarite's contact with a corpse.* He may, if he so desires, deliberately defile himself, and by this act alone he violates no law. [43] But once he is defiled, certain restrictions are placed upon him: He may not enter the sanctuary, nor offer up a sacrifice, nor participate in the Temple worship.[44] Defilement in itself is no violation; it is restrictive: it has the power to disqualify a man for cultic service. In brief, *contact with death removes a man from contact with the divine*—a theme to which we shall return. What is important to our purposes here is that in biblical/rabbinic legislation there is little fear or horror before death.

This is not to say that fear of any kind is totally absent. The Talmud, citing R. Levi, warns mourners that during the first three days after a death they must behave as if a sword were lying directly before them; from the third to the seventh day, as if the sword were in a corner of the same room; "from the seventh day onward, as if the sword were passing before them in the marketplace." [45] Here there is a projection of the element of fear, away from the dead with all its implications of worship of the dead, toward the living. From the Talmudic context it is evident that since death is retribution for sinful behavior, the survivors must be very careful lest they, too, sin and bring on further tragedy.[46] This is fear of sin rather than fear of death.

Death is the ultimate *tum'ah,* that which the Mishnah labels *abi abot ha-tum'ah*—literally, "the father of fathers of defilement." [47] And, in von Rad's felicitous phrase, "Every uncleanness was to some extent a precursor of the thing that was uncleanness out and out, death." [48] *Tum'ah* and the dead are shunned not because of fear, but because, as we will attempt to show below, death and its defilement stand outside the cult, outside of life, and ultimately outside of God.

It is not only in the negative sense, in the lack of horror or fear of the dead, that Israel differs from the ancient world. Israel's attitude toward death differs remarkably in a positive sense. It is apparent, for example, that biblical man faces death honestly and obediently and, occasionally, even with satisfaction. There is mourning and lamentation but, with Joshua, he says, "I go today in the way of the whole earth" (Joshua 23:14). Life was not an absolute entity in the first place. God is eternal and universal, but the life He gave to man is known to be limited. To die *zaqen u-seba yamim*—"old and satisfied with days"—is a kind of fulfillment.[49] The phrase "to be gathered up unto one's people" possesses certain comforting societal connotations: man is not alone, he is part of a people and a group; he returns to them.[50]

Abraham dies old and "satisfied" (Genesis 25:8). The description of the death of Isaac is almost identical (Genesis 35: 29). The same words—*zaqen u-seba yamim*—are used concerning the death of Job (Job 42:17), and identical terms are used for the deaths of David and Jehoiada (I Chronicles 29:28; II Chronicles 24:15). When Moses and Aaron die, there are no complaints about death *per se*: they are "gathered up" unto their people. Although Numbers 27:3 and countless other biblical/ rabbinic sources seem to tie death to sin, Israel realizes that it cannot master it, and is remarkably obedient to death and comes to terms with it. This is quite unlike the ancient religions which were so voluble and boldly mythological. Israel does not grant mythological power to death in any way since there is only one God. Therefore, there are no mythopoeic fantasies, rituals, or efforts to maintain a link with the dead.

The Relationship of God to Death

Fundamental to any world view of Israel is the all-pervasiveness of God, His oneness, and His universal dominion over life and death. How, in Israel's view, does God relate to death?

On the face of it, the question presents an untenable dilemma, particularly for the Israelite view of the deity. On the one hand, He possesses supreme power and rules the entire universe; on the other, it does seem that He has no dominion over death and that His power comes to an end at the grave. As proof of the latter view, some scholars have cited Psalms 6:6: "In death there is remembrance of Thee; in Sheol who shall give Thee thanks?"; Psalms 88:11-13: "Canst Thou do wonders to the dead . . . can Thy *hesed* be told in the grave . . . can Thy wonder be known in the darkness"; Isaiah 38:9ff: "Sheol praises Thee not. . . ."

God's absence from death seems to be so heavily stressed in the Bible that Mowinckel has been moved to remark that "it almost conflicts with the idea of the supreme power of God over the whole universe," [51] and Yehezkel Kaufmann declares categorically, "The realm of the dead in Israelite religion is godless." [52]

Of course, certain earlier scholars would solve the dilemma by arguing that in early Israelite religion, God was only one national deity among others and His realm was among the living but not the dead.[53] The moment of death was the moment when His jurisdiction came to an end. The dead could hope for nothing from Him, for He was powerless in that domain. Only later, they claim, did the prophets extend His power. Once He became universal, He was able to reach into the netherworld as well.

This view, promulgated by Lods, Deletra, and others, disregards several considerations. First, theologies and speculations about death tend to be very conservative, and late texts can reflect much older beliefs. Even the later prophetic utterances in this area are not necessarily reflections of a later development. Second, this view ignores the uniqueness of the Israelite concept of the deity.[54] Certainly, there may be apparent connections with other religions in that regard, but the total concept of God's relationship to death is uniquely Hebraic. Obviously, there is nothing in Israel's belief that can remotely compare, for example, with a Babylonian god of death like Nergal. Although this deity has the power to restore life, he is primarily a violent god who kills and who rules the underworld.[55] Israelite thought has no specialized deities for death, and in the Bible there are neither death motifs nor participatory rites in the suffering of a dying god.[56]

It must be pointed out that anthropologically oriented scholarship, which automatically relegates so-called "earlier" religious thought to a position inferior to "later" thought, is guilty of utilizing an unreliable evolutionary hypothesis in the area of religious belief and practice—a hypothesis which one scholar finds partially responsible for the basic fallacy apparent in most of the discussions of the biblical concept of death.[57]

The dilemma of God's supreme power versus His apparent lack of dominion over death may not be a real one. The passages which seem to support a cessation of God's activity at the grave have been misread somewhat, and Mowinckel, for one, errs in his view of a God who is absent from death. God is present in death, but only in life can man have a meaningful relationship with the God of life. The desacralization of death removes man from contact with the Divine, but it is certainly recognized that He ultimately rules the underworld since He is the supreme force in the universe. Psalms 139:8 affirms the presence of God everywhere, even in Sheol. Similar ideas are expressed in Psalms 33:7, 95:4, 55:15; Job 26:6, 11:7-8, 12:22; Proverbs 15:11; Hosea 13:14; Isaiah 7:11; Deuteronomy 32:22. The dead cannot praise God, not because God is unable to be present in death, but because those without life can have no relationship with Him.[58] R. Joḥanan expresses this idea very succinctly. Citing Psalms 88:6, "Among the dead I am free . . ." he interprets: "Once a man is dead, he is free from fulfilling the commandments." [59] And in Shabbat 30a the sages say: "As soon as a man dies he is restrained from [the practice of] Torah and good deeds." The dead cannot serve God.[60]

In Israelite thought, it is death itself, not the spirit of the dead, which is considered to be the threat. The threat is this: Death removes the Israelite, not only from the realm of life, but from God, who wishes to work within the context of life.[61]

The Cult of the Dead and Biblical/Rabbinic Legislation

The rigorous legislation concerning the cult of the dead offers further insight into the biblical/rabbinic view of death, a view through which death is radically and consciously demythologized and desacralized. Death is seen to be completely outside the cultic sphere of God. As von Rad puts it, "What is astonishing is the way in which this mysterious world [death] is entirely divested of its sacred character." [62]

It is important to note that the Bible does not deny that the dead have powers of communication. The incident in I Samuel 28 concerning the woman of Endor is but one example.[63] Similarly, Isaiah 29:4 evidently refers to the ability of the dead to speak: "and . . . thy voice shall be an '*ob* out of the ground." But though the power of the dead is not denied, human recourse to that power is stringently prohibited.[64] There is, for example, no biblical evidence for the practice of leaving food for the dead as a sacrificial meal for one's ancestors. And Deuteronomy 26:14, in fact, explicitly forbids the use of food of the Second Tithe for a dead man's burial needs.

Rabbinic literature also seems to admit the possibility of communication between the living and the dead. Thus, "Rab went out to the grave and did what he did," [65] which Rashi explains: "He knew the incantations [*lilḥosh*] on the graves and how to understand, from each grave, the specific cause of death." That is, he was able to understand whether each one had or had not died before his time. Berakhot 18b relates that a man spent the night in a cemetery and heard two spirits conversing with one other. It also records the conversation of a dead woman with a living man. The woman's spirit asks the man to request her living mother to send the dead woman a comb and a tube of eye-paint.[66] (In these two cases, incidentally, the dead spirits are prescient. They "hear from behind the curtain" [*meaḥorei ha-pargod*] about the retribution which is about to befall the world. And the spirit in need of cosmetics knows who is going to die on the morrow.)

The Talmud states that the dead man knows what is said in

his presence, at least until there is decomposition; after decomposition, the righteous dead cannot be brought back through necromancy. Samuel, who was certainly righteous, was raised from the dead at Endor only because this occurred within twelve months of his death, before the decomposition of his flesh.[67]

The dead have the power to harm those who disturb them unduly, and the ancestors have power and can speak to the living. The Talmud recalls that Caleb went to Hebron to the grave of the Patriarchs and prayed, "My fathers, ask mercy for me." [68]

Rabbinic literature, then, like the Bible, recognizes that the dead have certain powers. But rabbinic legislation echoes the biblical abhorrence at the use of those powers, and is particularly severe in regard to cults of the dead.

Necromancers and Cults of the Dead

The rabbinic amplification of Leviticus 19:31 concerning the prohibition of *'oboth* and *yidde'onim,* is a particularly instructive example of the rabbinic outlook on cults of the dead. The Mishnah[69] defines "master of 'ob" (*ba'al 'ob*) as the pithom, "who speaks from his armpit." (Greek πύθων , "ventriloquist, necromancer.") The *yidde'oni* ("wizard") is "one who speaks from his mouth." From the context it is clear that the Mishnah refers to the ability to make the dead speak in this fashion. "These two are stoned," continues the Mishnah, "whilst he who consults them [the dead]—*doresh el hametim*—transgresses a formal prohibition"; which is to say that mere enquiry of any sort of the dead, while not carrying a specific death penalty, is nevertheless also prohibited in Leviticus 19:31.[70] The Talmud in Keritot 2a contains a similar listing of those death cultists who are punishable by execution.

The Talmud's clarification of the Mishnah casts further light on how the *ba'al 'ob* actually functioned: "He knocked his arms" together in order to give the impression that the dead are speaking from within them; he "burned special incense to the spirits of necromancy" that they might help him in his sorcery; he conjured up the dead by "soothsaying"; he consulted skulls. In this context, I Samuel 28:13, referring to Saul and the woman of Endor, is a prototype of *ba'al 'ob*: the form that ascends from the earth to speak to Saul "settled itself between her [the woman of Endor's] joints and spoke." [71]

Midrash Rabbah[72] makes it explicit that this is the prototype. Referring to Leviticus 20:36, "And a man"—*'ish*—"or a woman"—*'ishah*—who have in their possession an *'ob* or *yidde'oni* shall surely die, . . ." The Midrash states:

> *'Ish,* this refers to Saul, and *'isha,* this refers to the woman with the *'ob.* It would have been better for Saul to have inquired of the *'urim* and *tumim* which are above, and not of the *'ob* and *yidde'oni* which are below. . . .

The *ba'al 'ob*, then, can actually raise the dead from the grave or, through incantations, can induce the dead to appear in a dream.[73]

As the Mishnah implies, the *yidde'oni* differs somewhat from the *'ob,* and the Talmud states explicitly that "a *yidde'oni* is one who places the bone of a *yidoa'* in his mouth and it [the dead] speaks of itself," the *yidoa'* being either a bone of a fish (Rashi) or of a bird (Maimonides).[74] The *yidde'oni* induces the dead to speak without actually raising him from the ground.

The Midrash from which the above quotation was cited even records in detail, the bodily position of the ordinary man who is raised from the dead by necromancy, in contrast to the position of a king when he is similarly raised. The same source discusses the ability of the living to see the dead as opposed to merely hearing the dead.

Just as the *ba'al 'ob* uses a bone for his necromancy,[75] so also is the witch of Endor referred to as *'oba tami'a* (*tami'a* meaning "bones"). The Talmud records the question of a certain Sadducee to R. Abahu, ". . . how did the *bone necromancer* (italics added) bring up Samuel by means of his necromancy?"

Isaiah 8:19 alludes to the kind of sounds uttered by the raised spirits: "And when they say unto you, Consult the *'oboth* and *yidde'onim,* that peep and mutter. . . ." It is from this passage, that G. van der Leeuw [76] derives the idea that the ancient Israelites conceived of the dead as birds. This is somewhat similar to the ideas in the Gilgamesh Epic (Tablet VII, col. iv) and Ishtar's Descent (line 10) and, quite incidentally, lends some circumstantial support to the view of Maimonides that the *yidoa'* is a bone of a bird.

Heidel finds possible additional support for van der Leeuw in Isaiah 29:4: "Thou shalt speak out of the ground, and thy speech be low out of the dust; and thy voice shall be as that of an *'ob* out of the ground, and thy speech shall chirp out of the dust." [77] However, Heidel disputes van der Leeuw's general argument about birds and, in so doing, presents an interesting analysis of the words *'ob* and *yidde'oni.* Unlike van der Leeuw, for whom these terms refer to the spirits of the dead called up by the necromancer, Heidel insists that they refer to demons within the necromancer that function at his command. *'Ob* and *yidde'oni,* since they are always used side by side, are synonymous, and it cannot be determined just how they differ from one another. [78]

Heidel's analysis might have been strengthened by a consideration of Sanhedrin 65a which makes a clear distinction between *'ob* and *yidde'oni,* both in terms of their method and function; and both Heidel and van der Leeuw might have improved their argument about the actual abode of the *'ob*—is it *within* the necromancer or brought up from the dead?—by taking into account the relevant rabbinic discussion in Sanhedrin.

In addition to *'ob* and *yidde'oni,* there is a third type of cult of the dead, alluded to in the Mishnah cited above: *doresh el hametim*—"consulter of the dead." Based on Deuteronomy 18:10-11 where *'ob, yidde'oni* and *doresh el hametim* are all in the same verse, *doresh el hametim* is defined as "one who starves himself and spends the night among the graves," [79] so that a *ruah tum'ah* will dwell on him. The *ruah tum'ah* is here unclear. Literally it is "a defiled spirit" or a "spirit of defilement." In our context, it is apparently an unclean demon or ghost who may help him in magic (Rashi) or in foretelling the future. It might also refer to the dead themselves who may answer questions addressed to them either at the cemetery or through dreams. [80]

The penalty for a *doresh* is less severe than for the other two, possibly because the *doresh* is not guilty of actually doing anything physically, and because he makes no attempt to raise the dead to him, but instead leaves the dead undisturbed and only "consults" with or "inquires" of them. As is true of any violator of a biblical prohibition, however, the *doresh* is liable to punishment by lashes. [81]

Typical of the rabbinic view of anything resembling a cult of the dead is the Midrashic exegesis on I Samuel 28:15. Samuel, having been raised from dead, says to Saul, "Why have you vexed me to raise me?" The Midrash Rabbah suggests a reason for Samuel's vexation: he was afraid of being punished as an object of idolatrous worship. Not only is the worshipper of the dead guilty of breaking the divine command, but the object of his worship, the dead spirit itself, may also be found guilty. The same Midrash, incidentally, lists this incident as one of the five sins for which Saul was ultimately punished, and apparently equates it with his killing of the priests of Nob.

In rabbinic literature, then, as well as in the Bible, any trace of the cult of the dead is a cardinal sin. [82] Israel is not permitted to recognize any other cultic sphere but God's—even if it means the apparent separation of the all-powerful, all-pervading deity from a significant aspect of human existence such as death (Psalms 88:11-13). The excision of the cult of the dead and the total desacralization of death is truly, as von Rad says, "astonishing."

God as Life, Death as Desacralization

It is not astonishing, however, when one examines the biblical concept of God as the deity of life. The Livingness of God is one of his primary characteristics. At the very beginning of creation, man is given a *nishmat ḥayim,*[83] a breath of life, and man becomes a *nefesh ḥayah,* a living *nefesh* animated by the divine *ḥayim.* The punishment with which Adam is threatened for eating from the tree of knowledge of good and evil is *mot tamut*—"you will surely die"; that is, the *ḥayim* that has been given to him by the divine will be taken from him.

The word *ḥayim* is almost always used in its plural form, which may be a grammatical underscoring of its intensive nature. The word *ḥayah* in Semitic languages may refer to a muscular tension, as opposed to death.[84] "To live is more than to be," and life is known by its manifestations. Deuteronomy 12:23—"the blood is the *nefesh*"—identifies life with blood or breath. Life is force or power, and anything that detracts from this force or power, be it weakness, sickness, imprisonment, or oppression by enemies is a relative death. In rabbinic literature this concept even has legal implications. A thief who steals a fat animal and causes it to become lean by starving it is liable, because of this argument, to additional payments from that moment on: "What is the difference whether you killed it altogether or only half killed it?" [85]

Death is described in the Bible as an "emptying out," which is to say that it is a losing of one's potential and one's strength. I

Samuel 25:37, *vayamat libo*—"and his heart died"—indicates weakness. Similar instances are found in Genesis 25:18, I Kings 17:21, Jonah 21:3, and Ecclesiastes 12:7. In the words of one scholar, "A man's *nefesh* departs at death . . . in the sense that his life ebbs away, leaving a condition of utter weakness or lifelessness. . . . Death can described as the weakest form of life." [86]

Ḥayim is the greatest good. It is a source of light, joy, pleasure (Psalms 56:14), and is given to the man who follows God (Ezekiel 33:15). It is a gift of which man must be worthy (Psalms 34:13-15). The Talmud, echoing this emphasis on life, insists that the saving of life supersedes all but three of the divine commandments.[87]

Throughout the Bible, *ḥayim* is almost synonymous with God. The goodness of God can only be witnessed in the *erez ha-ḥayim* (Psalms 27:13, 116:9, Isaiah 38:11); one walks before Him in the *'or ha-ḥayim,* "the light of life" (Psalms 56:14); fear of Him is the source of *ḥayim* (Proverbs 14:27); those who find Him find *ḥayim* (Proverbs 8:35); those who do justice walk in His statute of *ḥayim* (Ezekiel 33:15).

The Lord is explicitly the *Elo-him ḥayim* five times in the Bible, and He is *El ḥai* eight times. In these contexts He is the Lord who speaks from the fire (Deuteronomy 5:21); the universal sovereign Who causes the earth to tremble (Jeremiah 10:10); the speaking Lord of Hosts unknown to false prophets (Jeremiah 23:36); He who drives out the heathen tribes from the land.

When the Psalmist has reached the nadir of human existence, he reaches out for the zenith of all life, *El ḥai,* for whom he thirsts (Psalms 42:3) and for whom his heart and flesh sing (Psalms 84:13). Instead of being referred to as the people which is not God's people, Israel shall be known by the directly opposite appellation: *bene El ḥai*—"children of the Living *El.*"

The oath which is most widely used in the Bible by man is

that which swears by the life of God. This is found over thirty-six times. God swears by His own livingness over seventeen times: *hai 'ani*—"I live," or, "as I live." In general, the term *hayim* is used over thirteen times as distinctive from death or as contrasted to death.

When strange gods are ridiculed, it is their lifelessness that is held up to ridicule in contrast to the Living God (I Kings 18:26; Isaiah 42:19-21, 44:12-21; Psalms 115:5-7; see also, Psalms 106:27, with the reading of 'Abot 3:3). *Elo-him hayim,* according to one scholar, refers to the fact that God does not die, in contradiction to the pagan gods who die and are resurrected.[88]

The Lord of *hayim,* in brief, is not simply a Lord Who exists, but one Who is an active Force and Power. This activity is an echo of the actional nature of Hebrew thought and language, which is "dynamic, vigorous, passionate, and . . . explosive in kind," just as "the ancient Hebrew conception of man centers about action as against thought." [89]

That the biblical concept of life is actional, and not theoretical, is further illuminated by an examination of the word *nefesh,* which is used in the Bible over seven hundred times.[90]

Originally, *nefesh* may have had the meaning of breath, neck, or throat. Harry M. Orlinsky has pointed out that "the verbal form of *nefesh* (all in the *nif'al* form) is found a total of three times in the Bible, and in every case it means something like 'refresh oneself, catch one's breath' (not soul!): (Exodus 23:12, 31:17, and 2 Samuel 16:14)." [91] It later developed into a meaning in which the physical function implies something that is alive, such as breathing. The physical function of breathing or breath are the evidence of a person's livingness. Occasionally we find the original meaning, such as in Isaiah 5:14: *lakhen hirhiba she'ol nafshah;* and in Jonah 2:6: "water encompassed me *ad nefesh.*" This should not be translated "up to the soul," but "up to the neck," according to Orlinsky.[92]

Nefesh, therefore, is not translated in the ordinary way, as soul, because, in the Bible, man does not *have* a *nefesh,* he *is* a *nefesh,* "an animated being, a total person." [93] In Genesis 2:7 *Elo-him* blows a "breath of life" into man and he becomes a *nefesh hayyah.* In the same vein is Shabbat 152a: "The soul (*nefesh*) of a man mourns for him for seven days," which suggests that *nefesh* is the essence of a man. The passage *al nefesh met lo yavo* in Numbers 6:6 (and similarly, in 19:13) indicates that *nefesh* is synonymous with "man," and is not merely a single aspect of man. (See also Psalms 63:2, where *nefesh* is parallel to flesh.) All of this denotes a livingness and aliveness. Man is dust come alive. Death is understood as "the dissolution of this unit. Its aliveness is drained away." [94]

Rabbinic sources underscore the biblical emphasis on the deity whose primary quality is life and activity. "R. Abba b. Mamal said: The Holy One, blessed be He, said to Moses, *I am known according to my action.*" [95] (Italics added.) As an actional Being, God is the ultimate manifestation of the idea of *hayim* which is defined not conceptually but functionally.

The Rabbis also emphasize the livingness of God by vividly suggesting how He appears to man in various roles and functions. He is "like a king sitting on his throne; like an old man filled with pity; like a warrior doing battle." [96]

Further examples abound. The Talmud declares that the souls of the righteous are hidden under the Throne of Glory.[97] I Samuel 25:29 states, "the soul of my lord shall be bound up in the bond of life with God thy Lord." The Talmud interprets the phrase "with God" to mean with Him literally, with Him in His Throne. In any case, here we find another illustration of *hayim* equated with God.

In the Midrash Rabbah on Exodus 5:14, Pharaoh begins searching his archives for a reference to the Hebrew Lord, according to the rabbinic reading of Exodus 5:2: "I know not

God." Presently, he informs Moses and Aaron that he cannot find the name of their deity listed among the gods of the nations. Moses and Aaron reply, "Would you search for a priest in a cemetery? Those gods whom you have found are dead gods, but ours is *Elo-him ḥayim* and the Eternal King . . . and He created you [Pharaoh] and breathed into you the breath of *ḥayim*." In this Midrash, Pharaoh's inquiry as to what deeds God performs —*mah maʿasav*—elicits the dramatic and classic description of the actional God. Citing the actional passages in Isaiah 51:13, Psalms 29:7, and I Kings 19:11, the Midrash continues:

> His bow is of fire, His arms are flames. His spear is a torch, His shield is the clouds, His sword is lightning. He forms mountains and hills (Amos 4:13), covers mountains with grass, brings down rain and dew, causes plants to grow; He answers those about to give birth; fashions the child in the womb of its mother, and brings it forth into the light of the world.

It is noteworthy that rabbinic literature had its own nomenclature for the Divine. The Bible uses the Tetragrammaton, *Elohim,* and the other divine names; and the Midrashic/Talmudic writers have added other names. He is referred to as *haqadosh borukh hu,* "the Holy One, blessed be He"; *shekhina,* "the indwelling spirit"; *ribono shel olam,* "the Creator of the universe"; *ha-maqom,* "the place"; and *raḥamana.* "the merciful." [98]

Perhaps most typical of the rabbinic appellations is *geburah,* from the word *gibor,* "mighty one." The *geburah* is the source of all strength and power. For example, the Mishnah speaks of the three major sections of the Amidah worship, "the *ʾabot,* the *geburot,* and the *qedushat ha-shem.*" [99] *ʾAbot,* "Fathers," is the section referring to the patriarchs; the third, *qedushat ha-shem* is the section in which the divine sanctity is stressed. The *geburot* section refers to His power over death and life. In Mishnah Berakhot 5:2 (and 33a, 9:2, RH 4:5), the power of God to cause

wind and rain is *geburot geshamim,* "the power of the rains."
This power is "on a level with resurrection of the dead," which
is the major theme of the *geburot.* And in the Midrash Rabbah on
Exodus 5:14, cited above, it is the power and *geburah* of God
which created Pharaoh and gave him "the breath of *hayim.*"

All this is perhaps an echo of Psalms 106:2: "Who can express
geburot of God?. . . ." But the Rabbis extend this. *Geburah* for
them is not only a description but an appellation for the Lord.
Thus: "every word *mipi hageburah* [from the mouth of the *geburah*
(i.e., God Himself)] was divided into seventy languages." [100]
Similarly, "What did Moses reply before the *geburah?*" [101] We
find other *mipi hageburah* expressions in 'Erubin 54b, Yebamot
105b, Megillah 31b.

For the Rabbis, then as for the Bible itself, God is the embodiment of life which is not understood in abstract terms but
is known as action, force, power, strength, might: in a word,
geburah is the manifestation in deeds of the biblical *hayim.*

The livingness of God is His fundamental and primary characteristic. Death, as the opposite of life, is the ultimate opposite of
God. God is the Lord of life, and while He rules death *and* life,
He consciously withdraws from death and separates Himself from
it. Death thus represents the absence of a potential relationship
with God. It is likely, therefore, that the biblical/rabbinic laws
of *tum'ah* represent not taboos, but a manifestation of the *ab-*
sence of life, which is to say the absence of this relationship.

There are, in fact, innumerable indications in the Bible that
tum'ah and God are incompatible. The general meaning of
tum'ah, of course, is, "something ritually unclean and unholy."
The Bible is constantly concerned about the need to choose
taharah, "purity," and to beware of *tum'ah.* Thus, Leviticus
16:30: "before the Lord shall ye be *tahor*; ye shall make yourself *tahor* because I am holy, and ye shall not make *tamé* your
souls." [102] We find a similar separation between God and *tum'ah*

in Numbers 5:3: "ye shall not make *tamé* your camp because I dwell among you." [103] In the same vein, the Talmud states that "*taharah* leads to holiness" and, ultimately, to the possession of the holy spirit.[104]

Chapter Three

Categories of Tum'ah Defilement: Law as Idea

An examination of the specific legislation concerning *tum'ah* defilement may shed further light on our understanding of the divine separation from the netherworld and the resultant desacralization of death.

There are three major categories of biblical *tum'ah* defilement.

1. *Tum'ah* of the dead.
    a. A dead human being carries the highest form of *tum'ah* and is the ultimate category of defilement, *abi aboth hatum'ah*,[105] (which means literally, "the father of fathers of defilement"),[106] contact with which renders the person a *tamé met*, "defiled of the dead," a defilement which lasts for seven days.
    b. Carrion, or *nebelah*, contact with which renders the person *tamé* until sunset and immersion.[107]
    c. Certain creeping things which have died—*tum'at sherez* —[108] contact with which also defiles until evening.
2. *Tum'ah* because of performance of certain purification rituals.
    a. Those who prepare the ritual of the Red Heifer (ex-

plained below), and those who send out the Scapegoat (*sa-'ir la-'azazel*), themselves become *tamé* (Leviticus 16:5 ff.).

b. He who burns the Red Heifer and sprinkles ashes and water on the defiled man himself becomes defiled (Numbers 19).

3. *Tum'ah* of one's own body, such as seminal, menstrual, or gonorrheaic emissions (including *tum'ah* of a woman after childbirth); and *tum'ah* because of a leprous condition.[109]

In all these cases, including *tum'ah* of the leper, defilement is transmitted by touching or carrying something which is already *tamé*. Vessels that have come into contact with the dead or were under the same covering or were in contact with dead creeping things themselves become *tamé* and can render others *tamé*. Almost any type of vessel or clothing, other than those made of stone or earthenware, can receive *tum'ah* in this way.[110] Liquids may also become *tamé*.

Tum'ot have various degrees of "intensity." The *ab hatum'ah*, "principal category of defilement," [111] has the power to convey its own defilement to a man or to vessels that have touched it. Still others are *rishon letum'ah*, "primary defilement," which can convey defilement to food and liquids only. Examples of *ab hatum'ah* are creeping things, seminal emissions, an Israelite who has been in contact with a corpse, or lepers.[112] While most *tum'ot* convey their impurities through some physical contact, the *tum'ah* of a corpse has the greatest intensity and is unique: "Most stringent of all is the corpse, for it conveys impurity by *ohel* [113]—a manner in which none of the others defile." [114]

A corpse defiles for seven days, as do the various impurities of bodily emission, each of which is known as *ab hatum'ah*—a "principal category" of defilement. (This excepts the defilement of semen which, though a "principal," lasts only until sunset.)

While these "principal categories of defilement" are themselves already defiled for seven days, they do not convey a seven-day defilement to others. But a human corpse is not merely a "principal" : it is *abi abot*—the "ultimate category"—and possesses the highest power of defiling. Thus, a corpse is considered to be the ultimate source and the most intense type of defilement. As such, he who is in actual or "overshadowing" (*ohel*) contact with a corpse becomes a "principal" and is himself impure for seven days.[115]

The following facts shoud also be noted:

a. Those things that are in the ocean are considered *tahor*— "pure"—and cannot become defiled; thus, vessels made of marine animals or their parts cannot become defiled.

b. Vessels made of stone (*abanim*), or baked ordure (*galalim*), cannot become *tamé* and are always *tahor*.

c. The following can become *tamé*: vessels of leather, boneware, metal, wood, clay, clothes, sacks.[116]

d. Food (for human consumption) can become *tamé* if it has been in contact with specific liquids such as water, dew, oil, wine, milk, blood, or honey.[117]

Once an individual has become defiled, he is in need of *taharah* —"cleansing," or "purification." [118] There are a number of ways by which this is accomplished, varying with the degrees of intensity of the *tum'ah* itself. Intense *tum'ot* require a more intense *taharah*. In a *tum'at met*—"defilement of death"—or in certain bodily emissions and leprous diseases, there is a seven-day *taharah*, followed by 1) immersion in a specially prepared pool of water, and 2) the setting of the sun, after which *taharah* is achieved (Leviticus 15:16). For a lesser degree of *tum'ah*, such as seminal emissions (*shikhbat zera'*) or contact with carrion, there is a one-day *taharah* which requires immersion and the setting of the sun. Death defilement also requires purification by special rites of the Red Heifer and sprinkling of special mixtures, which are discussed below.

Several significant facts emerge from this brief summary of *tum'ah* legislation. As will be shown presently, the primary element in all *tum'ah* is death. In fact, the most intense form of all *tum'ah,* the "ultimate category," is a human corpse. This carries the highest degree of *tum'ah,* the greatest power to convey *tum'ah* to other things or creatures, and can convey this *tum'ah* in a manner more varied than any other *tum'ah.* Truly, death itself is the "ultimate category" of *tum'ah.* It is the epitome and prototype—the ultimate nadir—of *tum'ah.*[119] Furthermore, nothing that is alive, with the exception of man, can receive or become *tamé.* This is a significant exception and will be discussed below.

Death is the ultimate *tum'ah.* Death is also the ultimate absence of life. God, as we have attempted to show earlier, is the ultimate *hayim,* or life. Death, as the ultimate absence of life, is perhaps also the ultimate absence of the Lord of Life. It can therefore be submitted that the biblical/rabbinic concept of *tum'ah* has little to do with fear or taboo, but is a manifestation of the utter desacralization of death. That is to say, *the utter absence of God from death* is expressed in the concept of *tum'ah.* *Tum'ah* is the expression, in the realm of ritual, of what death explicitly states in the realm of the physical. In the physical realm, death is the absence of life; more explicitly, it is the end of man's potential for a dynamic relationship and connection with life. In the ritual realm, death is the absence of God; more explicitly, it is the end of man's potential for a dynamic relationship and connection with God. And wherever there cannot be even a potential relationship with life or with God—such as in death or in cases when God chooses to absent Himself from man —there *tum'ah* defilement enters.[120]

For example, the general godlessness of man is even referred to by the term *tamé*. Ezekiel 22:15—"and I will remove thy *tum'ah*"—is followed immediately by the contrasting, "and thou shalt know that I am God." Ezekiel 43:8 uses *tamé* to express the defilement of the sanctuary through sins, and Ezekiel 5:11 makes similar use of *tamé* in connection with the sanctuary.

It is death, however, which is the prototype of defilement. As the embodiment of the total absence of life and absence of relationship with God, it is the ultimate defilement. This is strikingly illustrated by the comment in Midrash Rabbah Exodus 38:1:

> Creator of the Universe, You demand that we shall be holy (Leviticus 19). Then remove death from us, as it is written (Habakkuk 1:12), "Art Thou not from everlasting, God my Lord, my Holy One (*qedoshi*) we will not die. . . ."

Clearly, death and holiness are not compatible.

Defilement and Death

What of those *tum'ah* categories, such as seminal emissions and the defilement of the leper, which do not deal with death explicitly? Are these simply hygienic taboos?

It is significant that in these instances, too, adumbrations of death—absence of life—are present. Whenever any constituent element of human life is lost, whether it be the loss of an actual limb [121] or the loss of vital physical fluids, such as seminal emissions or menstrual blood, there *tum'ah* enters. Even a certain measure of spilled human blood can defile,[122] because "blood is *nefesh*," that is, life; and absence of life defiles.

In addition, there is perhaps present here another manifestation of life. The seminal emissions may represent the seed of life which, now that they have flowed from the body, are no longer life producing. Naḥmanides writes:

> The reason for the defilement of seminal emissions, even though it is part of the process of procreation, is like the reason for death defilement . . . the individual does not know if his seed will be wasted, or if a child will result.[123]

R. Menaḥem Rikanati, a leading thirteenth century mystic, suggests that seminal emissions defile because the semen is like a corpse from whom the soul has now departed, "and the soul is the portion of the Holy One." [124] And it is worthy of note that, according to some views, a *ba'al qeri*—a man who has seminal flux—is not permitted to engage in Torah study before ritual immersion. Both the Jerusalem and Babylonian Talmud base this prohibition on the passages describing the revelation at Sinai where Israel is commanded to refrain from marital relations for three days prior to the revelation:

> A *ba'al qeri* is forbidden even to hear words of the Torah. What is the reason? Said R. Aḥa in the name of R. Elazar," Be ye prepared for three days, do not approach a woman" (Exodus 19:15).[125]

Berakhot 21b-22a finds the supportive passage not in Exodus but in Deuteronomy:

> R. Joshua b. Levi, said, How do we know that a *ba'al qeri* is forbidden to study Torah? Because it is written, "Make them known unto thy children and thy children's children" (Deuteronomy 4:9). Just as on that occasion those who had seminal emissions were forbidden, so also here.

According to R. Joshua b. Levi, one may not "stand before" God when he is defiled.

Even a verbal association with God is forbidden when one is in a state of *tum'ah*. "R. Nathan b. Abishalom says, A *ba'al qeri* may expound the Talmud, provided that he does *not pronounce the divine names that occur in it.*" (italics added). Mishnah Berakhot 3:3 states explicitly:

> A *ba'al qeri* says the words of the Sh'ma ["Hear O Israel, God is our Lord, God is One"] mentally [i.e., he does not articulate the words] without saying the customary blessings before and after.

It is evident, then, that seminal emissions are a serious form of *tum'ah*. As a result of this *tum'ah,* a distance, or an estrangement, from the sacred is effected. Similarly, a menstruating woman is restricted in certain ways, is a source of *tum'ah,* and is now estranged from the sacred.[126] Perhaps a rationale can also include menstrual emissions as representative of, and physically even synonymous with, the loss of the life force within the woman's body. Blood is, after all, the *nefesh* (Deuteronomy 12:23).[127]

As for the *tum'ah* of the woman after childbirth, here, too, we find an element of absence of life: once she gives birth, the mother is no longer producing, creating, and nurturing life. Birth is the climax of a process of life-sustenance which has taken place within the womb of the mother. The newborn infant now begins a life of its own—and is not *tamé*—but the mother's role of life-producing, life-nurturing, and life-sustaining now literally comes to an end, and perhaps this is why she now becomes *tamé.*

The Leper

As for the leper, he, too, suffers a kind of death. Rabbinic literature actually refers to the leper as "similar to a dead man." [128] The proof passage showing the leper's similarity to death is Numbers 12:12, which indicates that leprosy eats live flesh. In this verse Aaron prays on behalf of Miriam, who has

just become a leper: "Let her not be as one dead, of whom the
flesh is half consumed. . . ."

In fact, the very requirement to mourn for seven days is, according to one opinion, derived from this same verse.

> How do we know that mourning is for a seven-day period ac-
> cording to Torah law? "Let her not be as one dead." Just as a
> leper is quarantined for seven days, so does a mourner mourn
> for seven days.[129]

In fact, the very requirement to mourn for seven days is, according to one opinion, derived from this same verse.

type of paralysis, a marked change of skin color.[130] Even the
technical means of conveying defilement underscores the similarity of the leper and the dead in rabbinic legislation. It is
significant that a leper defiles by means of *ohel*—"tent overshadowing." [131] The only other type of defilement conveyed by
ohel is that of a corpse.

The purification rites for leper defilement and death defilement
are also strikingly similar.

Purification Rites for a Leper Require:

> *Cedar wood; hyssop; scarlet; two live, clean birds which are
> slaughtered over fresh water in an earthen vessel* (Leviticus
> 14:1-7).[132]

Purification Rites for Death Defilement Require:

> *Cedar wood; hyssop; scarlet. Together they are thrown into a
> fire consuming the Red Heifer. The ashes are mixed with
> water and kept for "waters of lustration"* (Numbers 19:1-
> 18).[133]

In general, rabbinic literature normally places the mourner

and the leper in apposition.[134] The Talmud analyzes the legal affinities between 1) the mourner, 2) the *menudeh* (one "separated" under a ban), and 3) the leper. The questions discussed are: does a leper deport himself like a mourner in the following categories: [135]

1. during festivals (he remains a leper—unlike a mourner, whose mourning during festivals is temporarily suspended);
2. restrictions on cutting of hair (he may not);
3. muffling his head (he muffles, like a mourner);
4. the wearing of phylacteries (unanswered);
5. extending greetings (he may not, like a mourner);
6. study of Scripture (permitted, unlike a mourner); [136]
7. washing his clothes (forbidden, like a mourner);
8. rending garments (he rends, like a mourner);
9. overturning the couch (unanswered);
10. working (unanswered);
11. washing himself (unanswered);
12. wearing shoes (unanswered);
13. use of conjugal bed (forbidden, like a mourner);
14. sending sacrifices to the Temple (forbidden, like a mourner).[137]

In a number of categories, then, the leper deports himself completely like a mourner. In the words of the Talmud, "A leper is like one 'separated' in some things, and like a mourner in other things." [138] The motivation behind the questions, as well as the explicit ways in which the leper and mourner are identical, underscores the conceptual kinship between the two.

That the *tum'ah* of the leper involves much more than hygienic considerations is suggested by several Mishnaic requirements:

a) a heathen cannot contract leprosy defilement; [139]

b) "any house may contract leprosy defilement except those

of heathens," and all garments may contract leprosy defilement except those of heathens;

c) certain skin signs which normally indicate leper defilement are considered nondefiling if they were present "before the Torah was given at Sinai" ; i.e., before the law took effect;

d) similarly, "those [signs of leprosy] which a heathen had when he became a proselyte" are not defiling; [140]

e) only houses in the Holy Land can contract defilement, in keeping with Leviticus 14:34: "When ye come unto the land of Canaan which I give unto you for a possession, and I put the plague of leprosy upon a house. . . ." Leprosy, according to the rabbinic reading of this verse, applies only to a house which "is in the land of one's possession." [141]

Now a heathen is not part of the covenant of Israel and therefore not subject to Israel's ritual obligations. But certainly the skin of the heathen is no different from the skin of the Israelite, and if the leper defiles merely because of hygienic considerations, this should have no religious boundaries.

It is also significant that a priest who himself is a leper may not eat of sacred food until he has been purified.

> Any man of the seed of Aaron that is a leper or hath a running issue shall not eat of the holy things until he be clean; and whoso toucheth any thing that is defiled by the dead or a man whose seed goeth forth from him (Leviticus 22:4).

Nor may a lay Israelite leper bring a sacrifice.[142] In Leviticus 22:5—

> Or a man who toucheth any creeping thing, whereby he may be made unclean, or a man through whom he can be rendered unclean, through any kind of uncleanliness (*yitma' lo lekhol tum'atho*) which he hath . . .

—the leper defilement is given the same weight as the other defilements, including the corpse defilement.[143]

One is therefore led to the conclusion that, like the other *tum'ah* legislation, the leper defilement transcends the obvious primitive taboos of fear and health. As Leviticus 13:15 puts it,

"He is *tamé*, he is a leper." That is to say, the leper defiles ritually, not hygienically.

The Red Heifer and the Scapegoat

The two remaining defilement types—The Red Heifer and the *'azazel*/Scapegoat—are also closely related to death.

The entire purpose of the Red Heifer ceremony is to purify a man who has become defiled through contact with the dead (Numbers 19). Thus, those who prepare the mixture of ashes and the water for sprinkling on the death-defiled man, themselves become defiled.[144]

There is, in addition, further evidence of the Heifer's connection with death. The Midrash points to the Golden Calf as the cause of death in the world. Exodus Rabbah 32:1:

> Had Israel waited for Moses and not perpetrated that act [the Golden Calf] there would have been no Exile, neither would the Angel of Death have had any power of them. . . . As soon as they said [to the Calf] "This is thy Lord, O Israel" (Exodus 32:4), death came upon them.

The Red Heifer, according to rabbinic tradition, is to be an atonement for the Golden Calf:

> A Red Heifer: Why are males specified for all communal sacrifices, whereas a female is specified for the rite of the Red Heifer. R. Aibu said, Consider this analogy: there was a maidservant's child who polluted the king's palace. The king said, Let his mother come and wipe up the excrement. In the same way the Holy One, blessed be He said, Let the mother of a calf come and atone for the deed of the Golden Calf.[145]

A related Midrash [146] lends added insight to the Red Heifer and its connection with the Golden Calf and with the leper: "The Red Heifer ritual is designed to atone for the Golden Calf *which was a leprosy of the spirit*" (italics added).[147]

What of the Scapegoat ceremony? Although he who dispatches the he-goat into the wilderness is not *tamé* to start with, the mere act of dispatching renders him *tamé*.[148] If defilement is connected with death, certainly the connection between the Scapegoat and death is not self-evident. However, there are a sufficient number of allusions to death, desacralization, and estrangement from God to set a tentative pattern:

a) The Scapegoat's death is starkly different from that of any other sacrifice. First, unlike an ordinary sacrifice, the Scapegoat is not ritually slaughtered. He is hurled to death and dashed to pieces. Second, the Scapegoat's death takes place not in the precincts of the cultic Temple, but in the "wilderness." [149] The Scapegoat rite, then, contains in it the critical elements characteristic of death; and in its violence, loneliness, and removal from the providence of God and the community of men, it is the death of deaths—the prototype of death—desacralized (not ritually slaughtered in the Temple), and estranged from God (killed in the wilderness). So utter and absolute must this death be that there is even a serious legal question as to whether or not the Scapegoat's limbs, after death, may be benefited from in any way.[150]

b) The Scapegoat is to be an annual atonement on the sacred Day of Atonement for the "failures, iniquities, transgressions" of the entire House of Israel. The public confession by the High Priest is an integral part of this ceremony.[151] The he-goat thus symbolically bears upon itself the entire corpus of Israel's sin, which is to say that it carries the full weight of the symbolic estrangement from, and absence of, God, which is sin. The Midrash Aggadah [152] on Leviticus 16:8 specifically states that the

Scapegoat "carries the sins of Israel upon it." David Hoffmann, in his commentary on Leviticus,[153] attempts to show that all defilement is actually a symbolic manifestation of sin, since sin is the cause of death. While it is debatable whether the Rabbis actually considered sin to be the only cause of death,[154] sin is clearly an absence of the divine, or a "missing of the mark" (חטא). It is, like death, an estrangement from God.[155]

c) The word *'azazel* for Scapegoat has no clear meaning. The term is used in Leviticus 16:8, 10, 26—and nowhere else. *'Azazel* is, possibly, an extra-human character, a kind of demon, and the Talmud connects it to *'aza'el* and *'uza,* who descended earthward in Genesis 6:2, 4, "and were the leaders of rebellion in the times of Enoch." [156] A Midrash on Psalms 82:6-7—"as one of the chiefs shall ye fall"—also refers to *'uza* and *'aza'el* who fell from the place of their sanctity in heaven.[157]

The Bible itself places *'azazel* in an antithetical position to God. Lots are cast for the two he-goats, "one for God and one for *'azazel*" (Leviticus 16:8). Ibn Ezra considers it to be an evil demon of the wilderness; that is, a non-god. Enoch 8:1, 10:12, 13:1, 15:19, refer to *'azazel* as a demon. Leviticus 16:10, 20, 21, refer significantly to the Scapegoat as *he-ḥai*—"the living he-goat"—on which the *Sifra* comments: "the 'living he-goat' implies that now he is 'living' but soon he will be sent to his death." [158]

In addition to these elements of death and estrangement which are inherent in the Scapegoat ritual, there is perhaps an additional allusion to estrangement from God in the Hebrew term used for the Scapegoat: *sa'ir*. Evidently, this term bears in it a hint of idolatry which is, of course, a major symbol of estrangement from the divine.

Thus, Midrash Rabbah Leviticus 22:5 [159] states: In Egypt, Israel used to bring sacrifices to the *se'irim*." Citing Leviticus 17:7, "They shall no longer offer up their offerings to the *se-*

'irim, . . ." the Midrash concludes that the *se'irim* are in fact demons. This is indicated by Deuteronomy 32:17, "They offered up to demons not to the Lord." That the demons of Deuteronomy 32 are actually *se'irim,* continues the Midrash, is suggested by Isaiah 13:21, "and *se'irim* will prance there." This is puzzling, since the Isaiah *se'irim,* based on the context, are evidently nothing other than ordinary he-goats. Yet the Leviticus Midrash evidently reads it as "demons."

This unusual Midrashic reading of Isaiah 13 is found again in Midrash Rabbah Genesis 65:15,[160] which translates Genesis 27:11 in a most extraordinary way: "And Jacob said to Rebeccah his mother, Esau my brother is an *'ish sa'ir.*" Normally, *'ish sa'ir* is "hairy man." The Midrash Rabbah renders it, however, in the Aramaic *g'var shedin,* "a man of *shedin—demons.*"[161] This is a surprising translation, since it transforms the normative "a hairy man" into "a man of demons," or "a demonic man." This is even more surprising in that it offers as a supportive passage the above-cited verse from Isaiah, "and *se'irim* will prance there." Here, too, the Midrash reads *se'irim,* not as "he-goats," but as something referring to *shedim,* or demons. (This is reminiscent of Yoma 67b, cited above, where *'azazel* alludes to fallen angels, and of Ibn Ezra's more specific rendering of *'azazel* as evil demons of the wilderness.) It becomes evident that the word *sa'ir*—the Scapegoat—contains within it certain clear intimations and suggestions of *shedim,* demons, anti-gods, or idolatry.

To summarize, the path from *sa'ir la-'azazel*—the Scapegoat— to *tum'ah* includes the Scapegoat's connections with:

a) the elements of desacralization and estrangement in its own death;

b) major sins (estrangement from God);

c) *'azazel* as a demon or anti-God (estrangement from God);

d) *sa'ir* as a demon or anti-God (estrangement from God).

That *tum'ah* should be a major characteristic of the Scapegoat rites is therefore to be expected.

Rabbinic Tum'ah Legislation

Until this point, we have discussed *tum'ot* which are specifically mentioned in the Bible. Even more instructive are the defilements which are not specifically biblical, but were added by the Rabbis. For example, there is no specific biblical legislation that imparts a state of defilement to an idol and its appurtenances. There is a clear allusion to this, however, in the passage, "Put away the alien gods in your midst, and purify yourselves, and change your garments" (Genesis 35:2). Basing itself on this passing reference, rabbinic legislation has added "strange gods" to the lists of *tum'ah*.[162]

Accordingly, the idol itself is *tamé* and conveys defilement to anyone touching it. Similar defilements are placed on those who bring the offerings, on the offerings themselves, and on any wine libations.

No reason is given for these rabbinic extensions of *tum'ah*. They do, of course, typify the rabbinic as well as biblical revulsion toward idolatry in any form. In keeping with our hypothesis, the concept of the absence of God and desacralization is significant. What is more desacralized than an idol? And in biblical language, what is more dead than an idol? "They have a mouth and do not speak; they have eyes and do not see" (Psalms 15:5). Who can be more estranged from the One God than those who worship idols? "As they are, so may their makers be, all those that trust in them" (Psalms 15:8). The contrast between the idol and God is explicitly stressed in the next verse: "Israel trusts in God." Significantly, the idolatrous sacrifices are referred to as *zivḥei metim*, "offerings of the dead," as in Psalms 106:38 and 'Abot 3:3.

All this is underscored by the biblical use of the word *tamé* in connection with idolatry. For example, Ezekiel 22:3, 4: ". . . the city that maketh idols against itself to defile herself," where the Hebrew *letam'ah* clearly refers to idolatry. The identical use of the word *letam'ah* is found in Ezekiel 23:30, and in Ezekiel 44:25, where it refers to the defilement of the dead.[163] Ezra 9:11 speaks of Canaan as defiled on account of its idolatry, with which "it has been filled from one end to the other in their *tum'ah*."

In general, the heathen himself, because he is closely identified with idolatry is known as a *tamé*. Thus, Isaiah 35:8: ". . . the *tamé* [referring to the heathen] shall not pass by." Similarly, Isaiah 52:1, "The uncircumcised and the *tamé* shall no longer come into you." [164]

It would seem reasonable, therefore, for rabbinic legislation to extend the lifeless, godless, desacralized, estranged elements of *tum'ah* into the realm of idolatry from the specific areas of death itself. In fact, this state of defilement in which the idolator is placed by rabbinic law has several practical implications. Certain doubtful emissions from heathens are considered to be defiling. And the requirement that the proselyte must ritually immerse himself in the same type of purification bath used by defiled Israelites is, in all likelihood, for the same reason: the heathen is in a state of defilement. For similar reasons, ritual immersion is required for vessels or utensils obtained from heathens.[165]

The other rabbinic defilement laws deal directly with death: 1) certain ploughed-over fields which may have contained graves; [166] 2) certain fields where a grave, now lost, is known to have existed; [167] 3) foreign soil (*erez ha-'amim*), apparently also because of unknown graves; [168] 4) *dam tebusah*—certain pre- and post-death mixtures of blood which may be rabbinically defiling.[169]

The word *tamé,* then, in biblical and rabbinical literature, bears the concept of desacralization. Death, as the highest form of estrangement from, or absence of, God, is the prototype of this desacralization. Furthermore, even a partial absence of life, such as torn limbs (above, page 35, and note 121), or seminal emissions, are tamé.

Chapter Four

Manifestations of Tum'ah as Estrangement and Desacralization

The Levitical food laws provide further illumination of *tamé*
as desacralization. This is particularly true of the eleventh chapter, in which the word *tamé* is repeated as if in a refrain.

Mary Douglas,[170] whose studies of purity are among the most
important in the field, presents an interesting resumé of the
various attempts and methods used throughout exegetical history
to provide a rationale for the Levitical laws. Citing Aristeas, Philo,
and Maimonides, as well as Robertson Smith, Driver, and Pfeifer,
she notes her dissatisfaction with all these attempts at interpretation. "The only sound approach is to forget hygiene, aesthetics,
morals, and instinctive revulsion . . . and start with the text."

She explains everything on the basis of "holiness," which indeed is fundamental to the biblical text. *Qodesh* is not merely
something set apart; it is also an idea of "wholeness and completeness." [171] For her, much of Leviticus stresses the physical
perfection required of sacrifices and of people approaching the
Temple. Perfection is also demanded in the social sphere. "An
important enterprise, once begun, must not be left incomplete."

49

Extending Pedersen's idea,[172] she concludes that "holiness is exemplified by completeness . . . [and] requires that individuals shall conform to the class to which they belong." And: The Bible "rejects creatures which are anomalous, whether in living between two spheres, or having defined features of members of another sphere, or lacking defining features."[173] It is not holy when different classes of things are confused. Thus, *qodesh* means "order, not confusion." In the dietary legislation, animals "shall conform to their class," and "any class of creatures which is not equipped for the right kind of locomotion in its element is contrary to holiness" and contact with it disqualifies one from Temple worship. Thus, anything in the water which is without fins and scales is unclean; four-footed creatures which fly are unclean; and anything which creeps, crawls, or swarms on the earth is unclean, "because this form of movement is explicitly contrary to holiness."

While Mary Douglas is rightfully unhappy with earlier attempts at interpreting the Levitical dietary laws, her own proposals, while unique, are somewhat inadequate and occasionally even erroneous. For example, it is not quite true that contact with an unclean animal "disqualifies a person from approaching the Temple," or that "to touch it is to be defiled."[174] Only when one is in contact with such an animal which is *dead* is one disqualified from the Temple. Furthermore, even a *clean* animal which dies without benefit of ritual slaughter renders anyone who touches it impure.[175]

Prof. Douglas's scheme does not account for the ritual differences inherent in living and dead things. Nor does her concept of unholy as disorder or confusion explain why it is that only contact with certain dead creatures disqualifies for Temple worship. Why, for example, should not contact with any element of confusion or disorder in the universe—sickness, dishonesty, destruction—result in similar cultic disqualification?

In addition, it is difficult to see just why a creature should be unholy simply because it is not "equipped for locomotion in its element," or lacks "defining features." A snake, for example, meets a number of Prof. Douglas's criteria for unholiness, and yet is not defiling. In any case, it is an accepted halakhic fact that only the eight creeping things of Leviticus 11:29-30 defile when they are dead, and that all other creeping things, such as snakes, do not defile at all.[176]

One sympathizes, however, with her unhappiness concerning earlier attempts at synthesizing the dietary legislation under a single scheme. The efforts of David Hoffmann and Samuel Raphael Hirsch [177] would undoubtedly meet with her approval. But Nathaniel Micklem was undoubtedly correct when he wrote that "these regulations are not . . . to be rationalized, their origins . . . go back beyond history." [178]

Perhaps, however, our thesis that *tum'ah* is essentially an absence of life and God, and is thus a metaphor for estrangement and desacralization, can be useful in understanding the frequent use of *tamé* in the dietary regulations of Leviticus 11. The term *tamé* here is not the defiling *tamé* of the dead who defile upon contact. He who eats forbidden food does not become defiled; no post-defilement purification is necessary if such food is eaten.[179] The offender has violated a negative commandment and as such may be punished by lashes.[180] The term *tamé* used in connection with forbidden foods, then, applies to these foods the pristine, metaphorical meaning of *tamé* as "something desacralized." The term *tamé* is an intensely pejorative one in connection with foods, underscoring their undesirability. *Tamé* used in this sense means that one shall not eat of these foods because they are desacralized, undivine, sacrally unfit. There is nothing intrinsically abominable or defiling about a pig. It is a creature like all creatures. But, says God in effect, I have forbidden it to you, and you are to consider it an abomination; [181] it is alien and removed totally from you, and sacrally unfit: *tamé hu lak-hem*: [182] they are, for *you,* desacralized and strange—echoing the desacralization and estrangement of the highest *tum'ah* of the dead.

No reason is given by the biblical text as to why certain foods are *tamé* and others are not. Our purpose here, however, is not to develop a rationale for the dietary laws; rather, it is to suggest that the term *tamé* in these dietary sections is best understood when we apply to it the pristine meaning of *tamé* as estrangement and unsacred.

Although the Levitical laws state no explicit reason for the food restrictions, it is significant that they do contain one implied rationale given to it by the text itself. Verse 45, immediately following the food lists, states, "you shall be holy (*qadosh*) because I am *qadosh.*" The holiness of God thus becomes the underlying motif for the dietary restrictions. Israel must refrain from certain foods which are *tamé* and by so doing Israel becomes *qadosh* just as God is *qadosh.*

Significant also is the juxtaposition of the dietary restrictions with the laws of the *ba'al ob* and *yidde'oni* (Leviticus 20:27). There is, on the face of it, no apparent connection between the laws of food and the *ba'al ob.* But in our scheme there is an intrinsic connection: both are *tum'ot* of the same nature, *tum'ot* of desacralization. One desacralizes through contact with the netherworld of the dead, and the other, through forbidden foods.

A detailed analysis of Leviticus 11:43-45 reveals very clearly the stark contrast between *tum'ah* and God's *qedushah.* Specifically, verse 43 is in perfect parallel with verse 44, "and you shall sanctify yourself and you shall be holy." The beginning of v. 44, "for I am God," is parallel to the middle of v. 44, "for I am holy"; the end of v. 44, "and you shall not defile yourselves," is again followed by "for I am God," of v.45, which is again followed by, "and you shall be holy." In each case, "I am God" follows the prohibition against *tum'ah,* and "I am holy" follows the command to be holy.

All this is further indication of *tamé* as the opposite, or absence of, God.

God as Qadosh in Biblical and Post-Biblical Texts

Tamé is not only opposite of God, but of every manifestation of God, especially His *miqdash,* His sanctuary. And when a *miqdash* reaches the lowest depths of impurity, the natural descriptive word used is *tamé.* Thus, Ezekiel 5:11: "My sanctuary (*miqdashi*) have you defiled (*tim'eta*)"; [183] and Ezekiel 23:38: *"tim'u et miqdashi."* Similarly, when Israel rebels against God, it is God's Holy Name which is defiled by *tum'ah.* Ezekiel 43:8 *"vetim'u et shem qadshi,* they have defiled My Holy Name...."

Even more explicit about the special nature of *qedushah* is Numbers 6:6. The Nazarite may not come in contact with the dead because the Nazarite is *qadosh* to God and, clearly, death is the direct opposite of *qadosh.* This concept is repeated in Numbers 5:3: "Ye shall not make *tamé* your camp for I dwell among you." God and *tum'ah* cannot dwell together. Numbers 35:34 is just as explicit: Israel may not render the land *tamé* "in which I dwell, for I, God, dwell in the midst of the children of Israel." The priest of God will die if he enters the sanctuary in a defiled state (Leviticus 16:2). Again, defilement and God are incompatible. That God is the epitome of *qedushah* is underscored by the fact that the root of *qdsh* is the major descriptive word for the the nature of God. In fact, God is called *qedosh yisrael,* the Holy One of Israel, no fewer than twenty-five times. In still other contexts, God is not only *described* by *qadosh,* the Holy; He *is* *qadosh,* the Holy. Thus Isaiah 40:25: "To whom will you liken me that I should be compared, says *qadosh.*" Significantly, when the total Otherness of God is stressed, He can only be called *qadosh* itself. So also in I Samuel 2:2, "There is no *qadosh* like God"; and Jer. 33:4: "His name is *qedosh Yisrael*." [184]

Rabbinic literature follows the biblical lead: the single most widely used appellation for the divine is *haqadosh barukh hu,* "the Holy One, blessed be He." This is found in almost every Talmudic and rabbinic reference to the deity.

In the major Levitical pronouncement about *qedushah,* Leviticus 19 exhorts Israel to be holy, "for I am holy"—"*ki qadosh 'ani.*" The Hebrew, unlike the English, emphasizes *qadosh* rather than *'ani.* The Hebrew says, in effect, that God and holiness are one and the same: "For *qadosh 'ani.*"

God is separate and Other. And if man wishes to achieve the status of *qedushah*, he must learn to imitate God and make himself separate and other from the world. Thus R. Elazar sounds a strikingly ascetic note in commenting upon Numbers 6:5 which refers to the Nazarite: ". . . until the days shall be completed which he has dedicated to God he shall be *qadosh,* letting grow untouched the hair on his head."

> Said R. Elazar, Anyone who fasts is called a *qadosh,* for it is written, He shall be *qadosh,* letting grow untouched the hair on his head. And if this one, who has afflicted himself concerning only one thing [his hair] is called a *qadosh,* how much more so is he a *qadosh* who denies himself the enjoyment of many things.[185]

God is so totally Other when it comes to *tamé* that He Himself refuses to use the word unless absolutely necessary. An example is provided by Pesiqta Rabbati's exegesis of Numbers 19:2. Pesiqta cites Psalms 12:7, "The words of the Lord are words pure as silver tried in a crucible on the earth refined seven times," and asks: "What can 'pure' mean here except that every utterance of the Holy One, Blessed be He, is one of holiness and purity?" Thus, we find circumlocutions in the biblical text in order not to use unclean words.

> R. Joḥanan pointed out that the Holy One blessed be He, spoke in a number of verses in a roundabout way, as in this verse, "And of the beasts that are not clean". (Genesis 7:2). Why all the extra words? (Since Scripture could have said *hateme'ah*— "unclean"—instead of using three separate words, *'asher 'enennah tehorah,*—"that are not clean.") The circumlocution was resorted to so as not even to use a word which stands for anything unclean, for every word which the Lord speaks is one of holiness and purity.[186]

Further examples are cited by the Pesiqta, concluding with: "The Lord does not let slip from His mouth any reference to uncleanness. Hence, 'The words of the Lord are pure words'. " [187]

The Midrash Rabbah [188] makes the same point, explaining the attempt of the Bible to avoid using the single word *tamé* by using two other words, such as *'enah tehorah*—"not clean"—by the well-known dictum: "*shelo l'hoẓi tum'ah mipiv*—"so that an unclean word not be brought forth from His mouth." [189] The Midrash on Psalms [190] arrives at the same conclusion, based on Proverbs 8:6, 8: "All thy words are in righteousness, there is nothing perverse in them."

The Priest's Sanctity and Tum'ah Defilement

We have seen that the most intense form of desacralization, the ultimate opposite of the Living God, is death. Death represents the total absence of physical life and the absence of the ultimate source of life, God. An examination of the laws of the priest should be fruitful in this regard. God may be invisible and not physically present, but the priest, after all, represents the highest form of tangible holiness. He is, in a very real sense, the representative of God in the cult, the very embodiment of sanctity. An investigation of his role and the legislation affecting the priesthood can yield additional insight into the nature of the defilement of death as it relates to sanctity.

That we are justified in viewing the priest as the earthly representative of sanctity is apparent from several sources, biblical and rabbinic.

(a) Deuteronomy 10:8: "God separated the tribe of Levi to carry the ark of the covenant of God, to stand before God to serve Him and to bless His name unto this day." [191]

(b) Exodus 19:6: ". . . a kingdom of priests, and a holy nation. . . ." "Priests" and "holy" are in perfect parallel here.

(c) In Leviticus 13, it is the priest who makes the final determination as to the precise nature of the leper's *tum'ah*. Verse 3: "And the priest shall see him and *vetimé 'otho*"— "shall establish his defilement"; verse 6: "And the priest purifies him." Commenting on Leviticus 13:2, in which it is specified that the leper be brought to the priest, the Sifra notes, "This passage teaches us that defilement and purification can only come through the priest." Even if the priest is unable to make the determination, a learned layman (*hakham sheb'yisrael*) determines the nature of the leprosy and advises the priest accordingly.[192]

Pesiqta Rabbati [193] reacts:

> In this world, things are pronounced clean and unclean by the mouth of a priest. But in the time to come it will not be so. The Holy One Himself, blessed be He, will cleanse and purify Israel from all their sins and from all their uncleanness, as is said in Ezekiel 36:25, "I will sprinkle clean water upon you and you shall be clean: from all your defilement, and from all your idols will I cleanse you."

Clearly, then, until that future time when the Holy One will cleanse Israel, the priest is the agent and surrogate of God. And, as Qiddushin 23b states: "R. Huna b. Joshua said, The priests are the agents of the Merciful One (*raḥamana*)."

The fundamental priestly legislation is centered in Leviticus 21 and echoed in Ezekiel 44. It is significant that the very first Levitical law refers to the prohibition against the priest's defilement by death (Leviticus 21:1). This is the theme of the entire priestly legislation: the priest may not become *tamé*. This is followed (v. 5) by various restrictions regarding the manner in which he may mourn his dead. He may not shave his head or beard, nor mutilate his skin. The apparent reason or purpose for these severe restrictions follows immediately, in v. 6:

> They shall be holy unto their Lord, and they shall not profane the name of the Lord, because the burnt offering of God, their Lord, do they offer up, and they must be holy.

The major officiant of God's sanctuary must have no connection with death, *because* he is God's officiant. This may also explain why a daughter of a priest does not have the restrictions of her priestly father, even though she is a blood relative and eats of the sacred foods. She does not come under the priestly *tum'ah* restrictions vis-à-vis the dead—"the sons of Aaron and not the daughters" is the only reason given.[194] Perhaps the reason is that only those who actively participate in the cult fall under *tum'ah* restrictions. The daughter, who is not an officiant because she is a female,[195] therefore does not come under *tum'ah* restrictions.[196]

When a common priest learns of the death of a near relative he must interrupt his Temple service and allow another priest to complete it; but he may not leave the Sanctuary until the other priest has completed it.[197] A priest who has killed someone, in addition to suffering the normative punishment, "may not lift up his hands to say the priestly benediction."[198]

The officiant and leader of cultic worship has special restrictions. The word *qodesh* is repeated in the priestly legislation as if in a refrain. The priest may not marry a harlot or divorcee or a *halalah* (child of a priest who has lost his holy status), because he is *qodesh* (v. 8). He must be *qodesh* because he offers up sacrifices. He shall be *qodesh* because God, who makes him *qodesh,* is Himself *qodesh.* Ezekiel 44:25 ff. contains essentially the same priestly restrictions.

The strict requirements regarding the priest's *qedushah* are pervasive in the Bible. We find, in several places, the scheme of abstinence and purification before entering the shrine—even for nonpriests. It is adumbrated in Genesis 35:2-3:

> Put away the alien gods in your midst and purify yourselves and change your garments. And let us go to Bethel and I will build an altar there. . . .

It is also reflected in the explicit purification demands of Exodus 19:10, 15, just prior to the Sinaitic revelation. And it manifests itself further in the "liturgy of entry" of Psalms 24:3: "Who shall ascend the mountain of God, who shall dwell in *m'qom qadsho*"; and in the formula of Deuteronomy 26:3, 13-15: "You shall go to the priest and say to him . . . I have cleared out the consecrated portion from the house, I have given it to the Levite. . . . Look down from your holy abode. . . ."; in I Samuel 21:5, where David assures Ahimelek, priest of Nob, that his men have been abstinent and are not defiled. Further shrine restrictions are found in Leviticus 21:21: "No one [priest] who has a defect shall come near to offer an offering. . . ."; Deuteronomy 23:2 lists further disqualifying defects, as does II Samuel 5:8.[199] So well known and widely accepted are the priestly restrictions concerning the dead, that the Mishnah reports that the people would mark grave monuments in blue in order to prevent any accidental priestly defilement.[200]

In fact, according to rabbinic tradition, Levi was already told in Egypt by his father Jacob not to be among those carrying his bier, since Levi was "destined some day to carry the Ark of the Lord, and therefore shall not carry the bier containing my dead body." [201] A typical story about the death of Aaron relates how the first priest had to remove his priestly vestments before his death, lest they become defiled.[202] And as long as he wears these garments, death has no power over him.[203]

A major recurrent theme emerges from this. God and his *qedushah*—and the priest and his *qedushah*—may in no way come into contact with the realm of the dead. In fact, the High Priest, unlike the ordinary priest, may not even come in contact with, or be in the environs of, deceased members of his own family—not even for his mother or father (Leviticus 21:11). He may not even follow the funeral cortege.[204] The priest, then, represents the *presence* of God and *qedusha*. Death represents the *absence* of God and the absence of *qedusha*: it is *tum'ah*. And *tum'ah* and *qedusha* can have no relationship with one another.

So rigorous is the Levitical legislation concerning the connection of the priest with death that apparently any hint of mourning practice, even when the priest is not in mourning himself, is prohibited. "Let not the hair of your heads grow long" (Leviticus 10:6) is translated as a general injunction against the priest entering the Temple with hair which has been allowed to grow long in the fashion of mourners. Ezekiel 44:20, referring to the priests, explicitly says, "nor shall their locks grow long." Sanhedrin 83a explicitly renders the death penalty (at the hands of heaven) to "a priest with overgrown locks"; that is, a priest who performs the Temple service when his hair has not been cut during the previous thirty days.[205]

Similarly, a priest may not perform the Temple service wearing torn garments, perhaps because this, too, is symbolic of mourning.[206] Furthermore, "a priest who is defiled through contact with the dead becomes unfit for cultic service until he "undertakes that he will no longer defile himself through the dead." [207]

The Met Mitzvah ("Obligatory Dead") and the Priest

The priestly legislation is quite remarkable in the manner in which the laws of *met mitzvah*—the "obligatory dead"—relate to the priest.[208] The *met mitzvah* is an unattended corpse. In the words of the Rabbis, it is a "corpse that has no one to bury him." [209] Who shall be concerned with its burial? The answer is that whoever happens to encounter the corpse first must bury him. And if the one who first encounters the corpse is a Nazarite, a priest, or a High Priest, is he absolved of this duty? On the face of it, it would seem clear that he who may not defile himself over his own family's dead should certainly be forbidden to defile himself for a dead stranger. But this is not the case. Biblical law does not explicitly mention the law of the *met mitzvah,* but an old rabbinic tradition, going back to the early history of Israel, maintains that even the High Priest must defile himself for the dead stranger.

Rabbinic literature derives this priestly obligation from the second half of Leviticus 21:11, referring to the High Priest: ". . . for his father and mother shall he not defile himself." The exegesis is: "for his father and mother he may not defile himself, but for a *met mitzvah* he may defile himself." [210]

No reason is given in the Bible or in rabbinic literature for the requirement that a priest (or Nazarite) defile himself in this case. Perhaps a rationale might focus on the idea that just as a priest's obligations for his family override the restrictions against defilement, so also with the *met mitzvah:* the unattended corpse evidently has no family to tend to it. Therefore, the first person to encounter it, whether priest or layman, now becomes its "family," with all the responsibilities of attending to its burial needs. There is perhaps an allusion to this in Leviticus 21:1: "The priest . . . shall not defile himself for any dead person among his kin. . . ." upon which the Sifra comments: "This means, as long as the dead is among his kin, thus excluding the case of the *met mitzvah*, who has no kin." [211] In other words, when the unattended corpse has no family at all, no one to tend to it, then the priest must step in. The overriding motif here, as is in so much of the rabbinic legislation on death and mourning, is that of *kabod habriot*, "dignity of human beings." A corpse must not be allowed to lie unattended, and if the only one available to effect its burial happens to be a priest, then so be it: the priest's sacred restrictions fall by the wayside when *kabod habriot* is at stake, for *kabod habriot* is in itself an act of sacralization. Even "the Holy One, blessed be He, Who is sacred and pure, extended His hand unto those who were defiled—because of Israel." [212]

The Talmud is quite explicit about this:

> Rabba propounded the question: As between reading the Megillah (Scroll of Esther which is an obligation on the festival of Purim), and attending to a *met mitzvah*, which takes precedence? Shall I say that the Megillah takes precedence in order to proclaim the miracle, or perhaps the *met mitzvah* takes precedence because of *kabod habriot?* After propounding the question, he himself answered it, saying, The *met mitzvah* takes precedence since a Master has said, "Great is the obligation to pay due respect to human beings since it overrides a negative precept of the Torah." [213]

So important is the *met mitzvah* that although one is forbidden to utilize accessories of holiness for lesser purposes, and they must be stored away, the Talmud records Mar Zutra's statement: "Wrappings of scrolls [even of a Torah scroll: Rashi, *ad loc*] which are worn out may be used for making shrouds for a *met mitzvah*, and this act constitutes their storing away." [214] And the

Talmud asserts that when Joshua parceled out Canaan to the tribes, he made the stipulation that a *met mitzvah* should be buried in whatever spot he may be discovered.[215]

The *Zohar* offers a very suggestive insight into the function of the priest, and ultimately into his role with the *met mitzvah*. According to the *Zohar,* death symbolizes separation (*pirud*), or a breaking apart of one entity into two: death separates man from God, and death itself was brought into the world by the sin of Adam. Death is also a *pirud* of man from God in the sense that Adam, by his sin, separated himself from God and the source of life, and was punished by the separation of death.[216] In the words of the *Zohar,* "Death is a return of all elements to their original source." [217] The function of the priest is the opposite of separation: it is to combine, to bring together. Death, by definition, tears asunder; the priest, by definition, reconciles. As a matter of fact, Aaron, the High Priest, is known in Jewish tradition as the great reconciliator, the "man of peace," *oheb shalom*.[218] The priest's role is to attempt to eliminate separateness and apartness. That is to say, through his cultic role, he is to bring together mortal man and the immortal God. Death and the priest, therefore, are diametrical opposites.[219]

When the priest confronts an abandoned corpse—the *met mitzvah*—the prohibitions attendant to his own sanctity as a priest conflict with his function as a reconciliator. To leave the body unattended would avoid violating the negative restrictions against defilement by the dead; to defile himself in order to give final burial to the lonely body would fulfill the priest's positive role of reconciliator which, as noted above, is inherent in the concept of *kabod habriot*. In effect, the law insists that his role as a reconciliator shall in this case dominate.

This examination of the priestly tum'ah legislation thus underscores the concept that God and *tum'ah* are wholly apart one from the other. We have already noted (pp. 14, 55-56) the significant fact that it is only the priest to whom the anti-*tum'ah* legislation is directed. There is no biblical or rabbinic prohibition against a lay Israelite's contact with a corpse,[220] and he may even deliberately defile himself.[221] But once defiled, he is restricted from entering the Sanctuary, or from participating in the cult, until he has been purified.

Maimonides crystallizes this idea:

> . . . there is no absolute obligation to immerse oneself, and any one who wishes to remain unclean, and is *prepared to forego entering the camp of the Divine Presence for a time,* is at liberty to do so, (emphasis added.)[222]

Contact with death or with *tum'ah,* while itself not prohibited, has the effect of removing man, be he lay Israelite or priest, from contact with the Divine.[223]

God and *tum'ah,* then, are incompatible. Or, to put it more precisely, that realm in which there can be no relationship with God is the realm of *tum'ah.* For *tum'ah* is inherent where there is no life; and where there is no life there is no *qedushah* and no relationship with God, for *qedushah* and life are synonymous, and where there is no *qedushah* and there is no life, because God is absent, there can only be a void—a life-less, God-less, sacred-less world of utter alienation and estrangement which is called *tum'ah.*

Defilement and Sanctity: Patterns of Paradox

An examination of the *tum'ah* legislation reveals an illuminating polarity of sanctity and defilement, whereas in certain cases a pattern of paradox emerges between the realms of *qedushah* and *tum'ah.*

First, we have seen above that of all the varieties of *tum'ah,* the most powerful and intensive defilement is conveyed by a human corpse. Not an unclean or unfit dead animal; not an abominable, creeping *sherez*, which is described both by the pejorative *sheqez* ("an abomination") as an adjective, and by *t'shaqzu* ("you shall abominate") as a verb (Leviticus 11:10 ff.); not a living leper, whose festering boils and dead flesh are horrifying: none of these is the ultimate category of *tum'ah*. Only the human being, alone among the creatures, into whom was breathed the Lord's own breath of life, achieves at his death the height of defilement. And more: only the Israelite dead is the ultimate category. The heathen dead is not *tamé* according to biblical law, and does not convey *tum'ah* to others. In other words, only he who once was able to worship God and was himself able to enter the sanctuary and offer a cultic sacrifice and reach the outermost limits of human holiness—"Ye shall be holy for I am holy"—only he can reach the outermost limits of defilement.

Mishnah Yadayim 4:6 states it explicitly:

> R. Johanan b. Zakai said . . . Behold, they say that the bones of an ass are clean, yet the bones of Johanan the High Priest are unclean. They said to him, Proportionate to their preciousness, so is their defilement, so that nobody should make spoons out of the bones of his father or mother. He said to them, So also the Holy Scriptures, *proportionate to their preciousness, so is their defilement. The books of Hamiram* (secular writings; according to Maimonides, *Comm. on Mishnah,* loc. cit., the reading is "Homiras" and refers to Homer) *which are not precious do not convey defilement to the hands.* (italics added)

Without citing this Mishnah, David Hoffmann [224] makes an analogous point:

> Only those animals and creeping things can contract defilement which were created with man on the sixth day of creation, because their physical structure is very similar to that of man, and they differ from man only by virtue of the breath of the Lord. . . .

That is to say, even animals achieve defilement only because they are close to man in the scheme of creation. Those who do not become *tamé* are "very far from the form of man." [225]

A dialectical tension seems to emerge here. The Israelite, and not the heathen, can become *tamé*. Houses outside the borders of the Holy Land cannot contract leper defilement (Negaim 12:1), nor can a heathen (Negaim 3:1), nor can his house (Negaim 12:1), nor can his garment (Negaim 11:1).

Furthermore, the graves of heathens do not impart defilement of *'ohel* ("tent defilement") in the manner of an Israelite grave.[226] The reason for this is that heathens and idolators, because of their idolatry, are considered not to come under the rubric "Adam," which is the Pentateuchal designation used with the laws of *'ohel* (Numbers 19:14 f.).[227] The further one is from the cult and from God, the less does one defile, and conversely, those who are closest to the cult and God, such as the Israelite, are the most defiling and, in the case of the priest, most susceptible to defilement.

Once life is removed and death enters, holiness is removed and *tum'ah* enters. The void left by the departure of *qedushah* is now filled by the forces of *tum'ah*. These new forces of death and *tum'ah* are now, in their own realm, as powerful as life and *qedushah* once were in their own realm. *Qedushah* and *tum'ah*, then, are two sides of a coin. On one side, man combined with God (life) is holy; on the obverse, man without God (death) is *tamé*. However, in order to become *tamé*, a creature needs to have had the potential of becoming *qadosh*, that is to say, he needs to have been human and an Israelite. *Tum'ah*, as it were, is the obverse side of *qedushah* (see, Kelim, 1:5-6) and is given, once life is absent, the power which *qedushah* had in life.

That there is some connection between *tum'ah* and *qedushah* is hinted at by several instances where *qadosh* and *tamé* are used apparently interchangeably. Deuteronomy 22:9 states: "Else the crop of the field may be *qadosh.*" *Qadosh* is here used in the sense of something that may not be used. Similarly, Exodus 29:37: "Whatever touches the altar shall become consecrated"—*yiqdash* (see also, Exodus 30:29). Here again, *qdsh* has a negative connotation, in the sense of "something separate," or "hallowed by contact." Similar usages may be found in Isaiah 65:5, "for I am set apart from you"; Exodus 30:20, Leviticus 6:11, 20, and, of course, Haggai 2:12.[228]

In rabbinic literature, we find Holy Scriptures, scrolls, and phylactery straps conveying *tum'ah* to the hands of the person who touches them with his bare hands.[229] There is even a discussion as to whether or not Ecclesiastes or Song of Songs are holy enough to convey *tum'ah* to those who touch them (Yadaim 3:5), while Tosefta Yadaim 2:13 states categorically that the Book of Ben Sira, not a part of sacred Scriptures, "does not defile the hands." And we have noted above that the more sacred a scroll is, the more does it convey *tum'ah.*[230]

Even the repository of all holiness, the Sanctuary itself, is able to transform a man into a leper: Uzziah's unauthorized entry into the Temple is an example of the sacred defiling the profane (II Chronicles 26:19-20). And, of course, touching ultimate holiness can result in the ultimate opposite of holiness—death. The classic example of this is in Exodus 19:12: "Whatever touches the mountain shall surely die," the mountain having been made *qodesh* (v. 23).

This tension between *qedushah* and *tum'ah* finds additional echoes in rabbinic literature. In an exegesis of Job 14:4, "Who can bring a clean thing (*tahor*) from a defiled (*tamé*), is it not one (*lo 'ehad*) [or: "the Only One"; or "no one"].[231] the Talmud states:

> [This refers to] menstrual blood [which is tamé] and is decomposed and turns into milk [which is *tahor*]. So said R. Meir. . . .

> R. Johanan replied: The passage refers to semen which is *tamé,* while the man who is created from it is *tahor.* R. Eleazar replied: The passage refers to the water of sprinkling [Numbers 19:9] where the man who sprinkles it as well as the man upon whom it is sprinkled are *tahor,* while he who touches it is *tamé.*[232]

That this is not merely a capricious exercise in exegetical gymnastics is underscored by Midrash Rabbah which derives additional paradoxes from the same Job passage: pure men have been born from impure men: Abraham from Terah; Hezekiah from Ahaz; Josiah from Amon.

> If he has a bright spot the size of a bean upon him, he is unclean [as a leper: see, Leviticus 13:12–13]; if it breaks forth on the whole body he is clean. None other than the Holy One could have decreed this. Or if a foetus dies in the womb, the midwife touching the foetus becomes defiled for seven days, while the mother is clean until the embryo comes out. . . . Who commanded this? Who decreed this? Was it not the world's Only One?[233]

In addition to the paradoxes of the impurity of semen as against life, and the sprinkling rite which creates both *tamé* and *tahor,* there is the Scapegoat ritual. The purpose here is to purify from sins, and yet, as we have already noted, both the one who burns the he-goat and the one who leads the he-goat into the desert become *tamé* themselves (Leviticus 16:26-28). The goat itself, however, remains undefiled. Similarly striking is the Midrashic statement that "he who touches the dead becomes defiled, but the corpse itself is not defiled." [234]

The paradoxes and tensions inherent within certain biblical laws are clearly recognized by rabbinic literature; for example, the Midrash [235] discusses forbidden mixtures, levirate marriage, Red Heifer, and Scapegoat as examples of statutes that contain this tension and inner paradox.[236]

Tum'ah and *qedushah,* then, seem to hover constantly over one another. It is not atypical, for example, that the very Mishnah in Kelim that lists the ten degrees of defilement is immediately followed by a list of ten degrees of holiness.[237]

The paradox of *tum'ah* and *qedushah* is that while they are ultimate opposites, they nevertheless seem to be in a mystical symbiotic relationship to each other. It is as if even two such basic opposites have origins in the same and single point, namely, God; but beginning from that common point, they move off in opposite directions—the one towards death and defilement, the other toward life and sanctity. Having originated in the one common Source, however, they each retain certain common characteristics. And perhaps this, too, is one of the possible readings of the elusive passage in Job 14:4, "is it not one"; that is, do not both defilement and sanctity stem from one Source? [238]

The paradoxes within *tum'ah* cited above are extremely suggestive. To these, the following can be added:

a) There is the requirement to remove shoes or sandals when in mourning,[239] and there is the same requirement to remove shoes or sandals when approaching a holy place, as in Exodus 3:5—"Remove thy shoes from thy feet, for the land on which thou standest is holy ground"—and Joshua 5:15.

b) It is forbidden to use a grave for personal benefit or enjoyment.[240] Similarly, it is forbidden to use any object consecrated to the Sanctuary (*heqdesh*) for personal benefit or enjoyment, according to the rabbinic reading of Leviticus 5:15, 16:

> When a person commits a trespass, (*ma'al*) unintentionally sinning against any of the Lord's sacred things, he shall bring as his penalty to the Lord a ram without blemish from the flock. . . . He shall make restitution for that wherein he sinned against the sacred things, and he shall add a fifth part of it and give it to the priest. . . .

Of course, there are other biblical allusions to this type of prohibition. Exodus 30:32-33 prohibits the personal use of sacred
oil; Leviticus 22:14 specifies the fine incurred by a lay person
who unknowingly eats sacred food; and an entire Talmudic
tractate, Me'ilah, deals with this one subject.[241]

c) If one weaves a shroud for a dead person it is, according
to one Talmudic opinion, forbidden to use it for any other purpose (Sanhedrin 47b). According to one opinion, the mere
designation of its use by the dead is considered equivalent to
having been actually used by the dead. Similarly, in holy matters,
the law of trespass (*me'ilah*) applies to a number of sacred
objects and offerings from the moment they are so designated.[242]

These illustrations may say no more than that certain precautions are to be taken with that which is wholly Other—in the
one case, the sacred, in the other, the dead. But considered together with the numerous Midrashic/Talmudic instances cited
above which specifically underscore the paradoxical commonality
of both *qedushah* and *tum'ah,* it is quite possible that they say
considerably more. Perhaps they prefigure the concept that sanctity and defilement, because they are ultimate opposites, are in
that very oppositeness similar in certain ways. Each one is an
ultimate force in its own right and this ultimateness may make
them, in some ways, rather similar in characteristic and function.
Is there an element of the sacred in death? For in the sense that
death and *tum'ah* are totally apart, separate, and other, do they
not resemble their opposite, *qadosh,* which is also apart, separate,
and other? And, again like *qadosh,* it is death which defiles those
who touch it, but according to the above-cited Midrash, death
itself remains quite undefiled.

Perhaps the most seminal—and ironic—of all the paradoxes
is this: death, as we have seen, is the embodiment of *tum'ah,*
desacralization, and estrangement from God. And yet death is
also the vehicle by which man becomes finally and fully recon-

ciled with God. In the concept of *mitha mekhaperet,* "death atones," the very act of dying is considered by God to be an expiation for one's sins. "Just as the Day of Atonement is an expiation, so does the death of the righteous expiate." [243] Mishnah Yoma 8:8 requires the Day of Atonement together with death for full expiation: "Death and the Day of Atonement expiate, with one's [personal] repentance." Mishnah Sanhedrin 6:2, records the statement which the court instructs a criminal to recite immediately prior to his execution: "May my death be an expiation for all my sins." In Tosefta Yoma 4:9, R. Judah says that the day of death is like the day of repentance, and expiates, as does death, for violations of positive precepts. There is further expiation when the body begins to feel the pains of the grave.[244] The Talmud inquires as to the purpose of burial, and suggests that it may be a means of atonement.[245]

What emerges here is the greatest paradox of all. Death is the epitome of *tum'ah* and distance from God; and at the same time, it is now the epitome of reconciliation and affinity with Him through its expiation from sin.[246]

Our further point: perhaps it is reasonable to suggest that this series of paradoxes of life and death, sacred and profane, has even more far-reaching implications. It is as if *tum'ah,* epitomized by death, were always present—hovering, as it were, in the wings while *qedushah* and life take center stage.[247] In the Judaic scheme of things, this is not necessarily a curse: death is part of the natural order of things, and "neither prophet nor priest can turn his back on death." [248]

In theological terms, this hovering death represents 1) the idea that *tum'ah* exists in order to be subdued by *toharah,*[249] and 2) the ever-present danger of alienation and estrangement from God. It is only the presence of God—His qualities of life and sanctity—which holds at bay the dominion of the forces of death/estrangement. As soon as God withdraws His presence, however, the forces of death, no longer held back by the presence of God, pour in to fill the void. In the words of the *Zohar*, "The forces of *tum'ah* desire to attach themselves to a vessel that has been emptied of *qedushah*." [250] Death takes over, and estrangement from God and *tum'ah* become as powerful in their own way as *qedushah* was once powerful.

The question of the power of *qedushah* as against that of *tum'ah* is suggestive of Haggai's question to the priests in 2:11-13. How is it that *qedushah* does not convey its qualities of *qedushah* by contact, while *tum'ah,* as we have noted above, can be transferred in various ways?

Perhaps an answer lies in a proper understanding of the essential difference in the status and nature of *qedushah* and *tum'ah*. *Qedushah,* as already noted, is essentially and uniquely a divine quality. Man may achieve some *qedushah*, but he is essentially *tamé*, and it is only because of the incursion of the divine into life that he can achieve some relationship and contact with *qedushah*. Even the High Priest will someday die and his body will become the ultimate category of *tum'ah*.[251] Death and estrangement are ever present. By contrast, the epitome of *qedushah* is God, and this is a permanent *qedushah* which never changes, whereas man's *qedushah* eventually crumbles into *tum'ah*, although—again, in eschatological terms—it ultimately triumphs over death and *tum'ah*.

Qedushah, then, can never be transferred or conveyed to anything else since it ultimately belongs only to Him Who is unique and alone and one. (It could only be conveyed to that which is *also* unique and alone and one, which is of course, a logical absurdity.) *Tum'ah,* by contrast, is essentially non-Godly and non-sacred; it is other-than-God. These other-than-God elements fill the universe, and *tum'ah* is therefore quite transferable. The inability of *qedushah* to convey its *qedushah*-ness, far from being a manifestation of weakness, is a declaration of utter uniqueness.

Tamé as Estrangement: Alternative Readings

While one is cognizant of the dangers of basing a theology on word studies, it is interesting, in the light of our thesis that *tum'ah* is alienation from the divine, that the *tamé* root is occasionally used in the Bible in the sense of "alien" or 'foreign" or "strange." Lexicographers such as Davidson (p. 522) render Zechariah 13:2—"and I will drive from the land of prophets and the *ruaḥ ha-tum'ah*"—as "a lying spirit: i.e., a strange, godless spirit." Amos 7:17—"and you will die on land that is *t'me'ah,* and Israel will be exiled from its land"—clearly uses *tamé* in the sense of "foreign" or "alien."

Furthermore, there are certain passages where a translation of *tamé* as "estrangement" instead of "defilement" provides significant and suggestive connotations:

a) Ezekiel 20:26: *"V'atamé* —and I defiled them because of their gifts" (which were offered in an idolatrous manner). Here, the translation of the *tamé* root as a force of estrangement would render the passage thus: "And I caused them to be estranged because of their idolatrous gifts. . . ." In fact, R. David Kimḥi on this passage renders: "and I made them *tme'im* and removed them (*vehirḥaqtim*) from me."

b) Joshua 22:19 reads more clearly if *teme'ah* refers to a state of estrangement: "But if the land of your inheritance is *teme'ah,* pass over to the land of the inheritance of God, where the sanctuary of God dwells, and dwell in our midst. . . ."

c) Ezra 6:21—"and the children of Israel who returned from the exile and all who had separated themselves *mi-tum'at goye ha-areẓ. . . .*"—is normally translated as, "from the uncleanness of the nations." *Tum'ah* here might more felicitously be a reference to the alien-ness and foreign-ness of strange soil.

d) Micah 2:10, a very difficult passage, is normally translated: "Arise and go, for this is no place to rest; because of
uncleanness [*tum'ah*] that destroys with a grievous destruction."
Since "arise and go" are the commands given by the invading,
or strange, soldiers as they prepare their victims for the journey
into exile,[252] *tum'ah* need not be rendered "uncleanness" : it can
refer to the strange and alien qualities of the invaders "that
destroy." [253]

e) Certainly Isaiah 52:1, by virtue of the synonym for *'arel*
—"the uncircumcised"—uses *tamé* as alien: "the *'arel* and *tamé*
shall no longer come into you [Jerusalem]". There are, in addition, several references in Leviticus where *tamé* could more
felicitously be translated as "a-place-away-from-the-holy-place"
rather than the usual "unclean place." Leviticus 14:40-45, in
which the priest takes apart a leper's house and casts the pieces
"outside the city" to a *maqom tamé*, provides an excellent
example.[254]

That rabbinic literature is not averse to reading *tamé* in its
broader sense is evident from the Talmudic exegesis on Leviticus 27:11: "It has been taught according to R. Johanan, 'And
if it be any unclean beast [*behemah teme'ah*] of which ye may
not bring an offering,' the text refers to blemished animals which
were redeemed." The Talmud then inquires,

> Perhaps it is not so, and it refers to an unclean animal. The an-
> swer is: When it says, "And if it be of an unclean beast, then
> he shall redeem it according to thy estimation (v. 27), the case
> of an unclean animal is thus already mentioned.[255]

The point of this rabbinic exegesis is that *behemah teme'ah*
—"unclean beast"—of Leviticus 27:11 is *tamé* not in the strict
sense of defilement but in our sense of alien and sacrally unfit
for the Divine.[256] That is to say, a blemished animal becomes

unfit for sacrifice; it becomes, as it were, desacralized. It is removed from the sanctuary and from God, and, according to R. Johanan, the Bible uses the adjective *tamé* to describe what is essentially a desacralized sacrifice. This is further support for *tamé* as a metaphor for estrangement from God.

In a personal letter to this writer, William F. Albright states that he is "at a complete loss to explain the origin of the word *tamé*." He suggests as a possible solution the Accadian *zamu* which means "to be deprived, to be in want, to be thirsty." He continues:

> The Aramaic spelling *tm'* has the same meaning as the Hebrew and can be derived from an otherwise completely unknown verb with initial *tet*. Or it can be, as probably in Accadian, identical with the homonym which appears in Hebrew as *same'* and Arabic as *zami'a*. Since the otherwise common Semitic word for "be thirsty" does not seem to appear anywhere in Aramaic it seems to be more than likely, from the etymological point of view, that the word "to be unclean" meant originally "to be lacking, to be wanting." (Incidentally, I noticed that the Latin word *satis,* "thirst" and the corresponding verb also have the double meaning of "thirst" and "want" or "lack.")[257]

In the same letter, he suggests that we "forget" about some very intriguing Egyptian parallels which this writer had pointed out to him. Thus, *temiu* in Egyptian hieroglyphs means "the dead"; *tem, temu,* means "to die, perish, the end." It is interesting to note that *tamia,* as in Berakhot 59a and Shabbat 152b, is the Aramaic for "bones of a dead man."

Albright's connecting of *tamé* with the accadian *zamu,* "to be deprived, in want, thirsty," is instructive. Theodor Gaster cites Babylonian and Egyptian funerary texts in which souls of the dead pray for water, and calls attention to Greek libations to the dead which are designed to quench thirst.[258] That there is constant thirst in the netherworld is shown in the Baal poem.

The food for the netherworld is mud and dirt. Gaster traces this theme of thirst in the Mesopotamian Ishtar myth, in Egyptian, Greek, and Roman literature, and in Avestan writings.[259]

It is apparent, then, that *tamé* has a certain connotation of lacking something, of being in want. It is also pertinent that, in an illuminating comment on Leviticus 11:43, the Midrash renders the odd spelling of *nitmetem*—which in the Masoretic text omits the normative *'aleph,* and is apparently metaplastic for the same word with an *'aleph*—as derivative of the root *timtem*—"to be stopped up." The verse would then read, "do not defile yourselves in them and become *stopped up in them.*" This would then be similar to the *nitminu* in Job 18:3: "we are stopped up (or stupid) in your eyes." [260]

A similar rabbinic sensitivity to the idea of *tum'ah* as more than ordinary ritual defilement is seen in Yoma 39a:

> If a man defiles himself below, he becomes defiled from above; if he defiles himself in this world, he becomes defiled in the world to come.

By the same token:

> If he sanctifies himself below, he becomes sanctified from above; if he sanctifies himself in this world, he becomes sanctified in the world to come.[261]

Tum'ah is an aspect of man's relationship to the Divine. In theological terms, what Yoma 39 says is this: if man chooses to estrange himself from God, God will react measure for measure. He will estrange Himself from man in accordance with man's estrangement from God. By the same token, if man chooses to sanctify himself (i.e., approach the Divine), God will, in the same measure, approach man.

In the same manner we might better understand the rabbinic

statements that "the righteous do not defile." [262] The weight of halakhic opinion would indicate that a righteous man, once he dies, conveys *tum'ah* in the manner of any corpse. Perhaps the Rabbis are here, too, using *tum'ah* in its sense of estrangement. The righteous man is never estranged from the Lord even after he dies. *Zaddikim b'motham niqraim ḥayim*—"the righteous even when they are dead are called living" (Berakhot 18a).

SECTION II

DEATH AND MOURNING: ESTRANGEMENT AND DESACRALIZATION IN PRACTICE

Chapter One

The Halakhah of Mourning

In the first section, Israel's view of death within the context of the ancient world was examined, and an attempt was made to describe how the existence of *tum'ah* legislation in biblical and rabbinic Israel leads to several conclusions: first, that absence of life is a key element in defilement; second, that death represents the utmost desacralization since the major element in the nature of God is life; and third and most important, that *tum'ah* defilement symbolizes estrangement from the Divine.

The second section will focus primarily on the post-biblical mourning legislation as a concrete illustration of these conclusions.

Israel shares with all of mankind specific laws, practices, customs, and observances dealing with death and mourning. In some details, these are common to all men; in others, they are uniquely Israelitic. In those details that are particular to Israel and have been formalized almost entirely into law by post-biblical rabbinic sources, is there a pattern of thought discernible which, like the legislation itself, is also uniquely Israelitic? Is there an implicit theology or a world view that emerges from a study of the post-biblical legislation concerning death and mourning? More specifically, does this legislative system support the patterns of thought which have been uncovered to us during our study of defilement? Does it tell us anything more about the estrangement and desacralization of death? This section will address itself to these questions.

The Israelite practice of mourning for the dead evidently goes back quite far into antiquity. The biblical Joseph, for example, mourns his father, Jacob, for a period of seven days (Genesis 50:10). Although the seven day period of deep mourning immediately following death is obviously a very old practice, the Talmud is hard pressed to find a definite Scriptural base for it. There is no specific biblical commandment to mourn for seven days, and the Talmud questions whether mourning for this period is a prescribed Scriptural law or a later rabbinic enactment. Genesis 50:10, perhaps, provides some basis for the concept that it is a Scriptural law; but the Talmudic discussant objects that one may not derive biblical obligations from events that transpired prior to the Sinaitic Revelation. Therefore, it is maintained that only the first day of mourning is biblically ordained, while the rest of the days are rabbinic but not Scriptural obligations.[1]

The basic principle of mourning is apparently based on the Bible. In Leviticus 10:19, Aaron says, after the death of his sons: ". . . and if I had eaten the sin-offering today, would it have been pleasing in the eyes of the Lord?" That is to say, since he was a mourner he obviously was not permitted to eat of the offering. And since the priest's mourning obligations for a close relative are the same as those of an Israelite, the passage clearly implies that the requirement to mourn a relative—whether of a priest or non-priest—extends, at least Scripturally, for an entire day.[2]

J. Ketubot 1:1 states that the seven-day period for mourning and for religious feasts were both ordained by Moses himself.

Elsewhere the Talmud bases the seven-day requirement on a combination of passages from Amos and Leviticus. Amos 8:10 states: "And I will turn your feasts (*hagekhem*) into mourning. . . . and I will make it as the mourning for an only son." Just as the feast in Leviticus 23:7-8, 34-36 lasts seven days, so does the mourning period extend for seven days, for, according to Amos 8:10, feasts and mourning are analogous.[3] Other rabbinic sources depict God mourning for the world for seven days prior to its destruction by the Noachide flood.[4]

The mourning period is divided into several major categories:

a) the period between death and burial;

b) the first day of post-burial mourning;

c) the first seven days of mourning;[5]

d) the first thirty days of mourning;

e) the first year of mourning.

These categories require certain practices, or are subject to certain restrictions which, as will be seen below, are germane to the thesis of *tum'ah* defilement as estrangement and desacralization.

Between Death and Burial: Laws of the Onen

The mourner is not subject to the laws of mourning until after burial. On the day on which death occurs, but prior to the actual burial, he is known as an *onen*.[6] The root of *onen* may be found in Numbers 11:1: *mith'onenim*—"lamenters" or "complainers"—and Lamentations 3:39: *yith'onen*—"he will lament" —and refers to the initial period of mourning when grief is at its deepest and most intense.

The laws of the *onen* represent a key to our understanding of death and defilement as desacralization and estrangement, for the *onen* must refrain from fulfilling the precepts of God. For example:

a) the *onen* is exempt from the wearing of phylacteries;
b) he does not recite the benediction before or after meals;
c) he may not recite the *amen* when he hears a benediction; [7]
d) he does not recite the required *sh'ma* prayer;
e) he is exempted from all positive biblical precepts; [8]
f) based on Leviticus 10:19, a priest who is an *onen* is forbidden to eat of sacred food. [9]

The High Priest, on the other hand, may offer sacrifices on the altar even while he is an *onen*. This is based on Aaron, who offered up a sacrifice although his two sons died on the day he was inaugurated as High Priest. He does not, however, partake of the sacred meat. [10] An Israelite *onen* is forbidden to eat of the first fruits and the second tithe. [11]

The apparent concern of the law of *onen* is that the *onen* should expend all of his energies towards the preparations needed for the dead, and that nothing—not even performance of biblical precepts—should be permitted to distract him from this one overriding concern. [12]

The Onen and Desacralization

On a different level, however, the laws of the *onen* present us with additional evidence for the concept of death as desacralization. The *onen,* experiencing as he does the immediate moment of death, represents the concept of mourning in microcosm: he has felt the pangs of death in their sharpest and most acute form. At this moment death is a most real and tangible fact for him. And it is precisely while he is an *onen* and is existentially experiencing death at first hand that the halakhah exempts him from performing the precepts—as if to say, *When death enters, man's relationship with God is temporarily suspended.*

From this moment—through the burial, the first seven days

of mourning, and the first thirty days—the mourner begins a process of gradual return. This is a return not only to normal life as a member of a family and a community, but to a normal relationship with God which has been severed by the presence of death. And at the depth of mourning, when the dead is yet unburied and, so to speak, still among the living—that is, when the bereaved is an *onen*—God, as it were, withdraws Himself. After burial, when death is at least physically removed from the environs, the relationship with God begins to reestablish itself. The meaningful interaction and relationship with God, from which the *onen* has been estranged by the presence of death, must now gradually become reestablished. That which has been desacralized must now be resacralized.

Post-Burial Mourning: the First Day

During the first day of mourning, the mourner is forbidden to eat his own food.[13] This is based on Ezekiel 24:17: "And eat not the bread of men," from which the Talmud deduces that the mourner's food must be prepared by, and must belong to others.[14] This meal is eaten not at the grave, but upon returning to one's own dwelling. There was, in fact, strong sentiment against permitting the meal at the graveside, probably in reaction to heathen ancestor-cult rites at the site of the grave.[15]

The Israelites mourning meal was known as *seudat habra'ah*[16] and is evidently very old. Already in II Samuel 3:35 we find that "all the people came *l'habroth* to David the bread during the day," after the death of Abner. And in Jeremiah 16:7: ". . . nor shall men break bread for them at their mourning, to comfort them for the dead; . . ."[17] The Talmud takes Genesis 25:29 ("And Jacob boiled *'adashim*") to refer to a mourning meal:

> This was the day on which our Father Abraham died, and our Father Jacob made a broth of lentils to comfort his father Isaac.[18]

Although no specific reason is given for the practice of the mourning meal, it is apparent that one of the purposes was to comfort the mourners and help ease their sorrow.

The mourner, if he wishes to do so, may fast on that first day and not eat of the special meal.[19] Some have supported this practice by citing Leviticus 19:26: "Thou shalt not eat upon the blood," which may imply that one should not eat on the day of burial.[20] The men of Beth She'an "fasted seven days" after the burial of Saul (I Samuel 31:13). David and his men fasted until nightfall when they heard of the death of Saul and Jonathan (II Samuel 1:12), and David would not touch food during his mourning for Abner.[21] When Judith became a widow, she fasted constantly, except on Sabbath and festivals (8:4-6). The Jewish army at Yeb in Elephantine described its deep mourning because of the outrage to their Temple:

> Know to this day we are clad in sackcloth, and *keep fasting* while our wives are like widows (referring to the prohibition against mourners engaging in "use of the conjugal bed," as we will note below). We anoint ourselves not with oil (see below on prohibitions against anointing and washing), nor do we drink wine. (Italics added.)[22]

Post-Burial Mourning: the first week

The initial seven-day period immediately following death and burial is the most intensive period of mourning. During this time, the following are prohibited in rabbinic tradition:

a. *Cutting one's hair.* This is based on Leviticus 10:6.[23]

b. *Washing one's clothes.* This is based on II Samuel 14:2: "And Joab sent to Tekoah and he took from there a wise woman, and he said to her, Do thou mourn and wear mourning clothes, and do not anoint thyself with oil, and thou shalt be as a woman mourning on her husband for many days." The Talmud [24] sees in the phrase "mourning clothes" a clear implication that the clothes she was bidden to wear were to be unwashed. According to one Talmudic opinion, washing of clothes itself is not forbidden; the prohibition extends only to the wearing of newly washed garments.

c. *Anointing or washing oneself*. This, too, is based on the above-cited passage. Moed Qatan 15b also cites Psalms 109:18, in which water is parallel to anointing with oil.[25] (It is interesting that the Talmudic exegesis here uses literary parallelism to prove a legal point.) That washing is normally a part of anointing is indicated from Ruth 3:3, which mentions them together: "Wash and anoint thyself." According to J. Berakhot 2:7, they are forbidden because they give pleasure. By the same token, if the mourner is unusually dirty, it is permitted to wash, but only for the purposes of cleansing himself, not for pleasure.

d. *"Use of the* [conjugal] *bed"* (marital relations). This is derived from II Samuel 12:24, concerning David and Bathsheba. The passage implies that she was forbidden to him prior to the end of the mourning period. A mourner may not take a wife during the mourning period even if he does not physically consummate the marriage. Betrothal, however, is permitted.[26]

e. *Wearing of shoes*. This is derived from Ezekiel 24:17: "And thy shoes shalt thou place on thy feet," which, for the Rabbis, implies that this is permissible only to Ezekiel but is forbidden to all other mourners.[27]

f. *Working* is forbidden, based on Amos 8:10: "And I will turn thy festivals into mourning": just as a festival involves a prohibition against work, so also is a mourner forbidden to work.

g. *Study of Scripture*. This is based on the same passage in Ezekiel. J. Moed Qatan derives this prohibition from Job 2:13, " 'And does not speak a word to him': even a word of Scripture."

h. *Sitting on a bed or couch*. This is based on II Samuel 13: 31, where it is said of King David that "the King rose up and tore his clothes and lay on the ground." Additional support is in Job 2:13: "And they sat with him on the ground." [28] It is interesting that there is no requirement to sit on the ground; he may walk or stand constantly. But if he does sit, it is not to be on a regular bed or chair, but on the ground or on a low stool. Related to this is the requirement to "overturn the bed," based on Bar Kappara's dictum:

> The Lord says, I have set the likeness of mine image on them, and because of their sins have I upset it; let your covers therefore be overturned on account thereof.

That is to say, man has distorted his divine image by sinning, and man's sin has brought on death.[29] As an act of mourning, he does not sleep in the normal manner.

i. *Muffling one's head* is now prescribed; that is, the mourner must cover his head and most of his face with a kerchief. Known as *pri'ath ha-rosh,* this is based on Ezekiel 24:17, which implies that a non-priest must wrap his head. The purpose here is evidently to make a mourner look like a broken and humbled man.[30]

j. The mourner is prohibited from offering a *greeting of well-being.* Literally, he may not "ask one's peace," as in Genesis 24:6: "Is it peace with him? It is peace." This too is based on Ezekiel 24:17: *he'aneq dom*—"sigh in silence." The mourner may not give or receive greetings for the first three days of mourning.

In addition to the above restrictions, the mourner has one further restriction—and for our purposes a very significant one. The mourner may not offer a sacrifice for seven days. "R. Simon says, the *shlamim* sacrifice (whole offering) is offered at a time when he is *shalem* (i.e., "complete") and not at a time when he is an *onen.*" [31] Tosefta Zebaḥim 11 states, "An *onen* is not permitted to bring a sacrifice for the entire seven day period." [32]

Post-Burial Mourning: The First Month

The secondary period of mourning continues until thirty days after death. Rabbinic law derives its source for this period from Deuteronomy 34:18: "The children of Israel wept for Moses in the plains of Moab thirty days;" and from Deuteronomy 21:13: "She shall spend a month's time lamenting her father and mother." During this period, some of the seven-day restrictions fall away while others continue. For example, the mourner still may not shave or cut his hair. According to Moed Qatan 19b, the requirement for hair to grow thirty days is derived from the restrictions on the Nazarite, whose requirement is expressly stated to be for thirty days. During this thirty-day period the mourner may not press his clothes,[33] or attend social gatherings, or marry. And, again significantly, he may not sit in his usual place in the synagogue.[34]

According to rabbinic law, the rules of mourning apply for these relatives: wife, mother, father, sister, brother, son, daughter.[35] Here, too, the source is the priestly rule in Leviticus 21:2-3.[36] Rabbinic legislation later added four additional mourning obligations: mourning is required not only for the brother and sister of the same father but also of the same mother, and a married sister from the same father or mother. In addition, a rabbinic injunction states that mourning is obligatory for one's teacher "who taught him wisdom." This is an obligation only for one day.[37]

Even if the deceased is a relative, one does not mourn the following: a foetus; those executed by duly constituted courts of law; those who have abandoned the publicly accepted way of life, since they have "thrown off the yoke of the commandments" and are not considered to be part of the community of Israel; and suicides.[38]

While ordinary mourning concludes at the end of thirty days, the period of mourning for one's parents continues, with decreasing intensity, for an entire year.

Mourning Practices on Sabbaths and Festivals

Most of the mourning laws do not apply on the Sabbath. This is based on Proverbs 10:22: "It is the blessing of the Lord which maketh rich, and sadness addeth nothing thereto," to which the Talmud adds: " 'It is the blessing,' is the Sabbath, while 'sadness addeth nothing' refers to mourning." [39] Moed Qatan 23b records a dispute between those living in the Galilee and those living in Judea concerning private mourning on the Sabbath. It is the practice to continue to observe mourning in private, while suspending mourning in public—such as during public worship—for that one day. The Sabbath is counted as one of the required days of mourning, since some of the personal mourning practices do apply to it. [40] The study of Scripture is considered a private practice and is prohibited to the mourner even on the Sabbath.

In public matters, no mourning is practiced on the Sabbath, even when the mourning is for parents. The mourner wears regular shoes on the Sabbath, does not have the obligation of overturning his couch, greets everyone, changes his clothing (so that he not wear torn clothes on the Sabbath), or at least hides the tear in his clothes. He also does not sit on the ground or on a low stool, out of respect to the Sabbath day.

Festivals are treated like Sabbaths in that mourning laws also fall away. This is based on Deuteronomy 16:14: "Thou shalt rejoice in thy festivals." The reason is that a positive commandment dealing with the community supersedes a positive commandment dealing with an individual (who may be in mourning). [41] Festivals differ from Sabbaths in one major respect: should a festival occur during the seven-day mourning period, the seven-day mourning obligations come to a permanent end, and need not be taken up again after the festival. After the Sabbath interruption of mourning, however, the "seven-day" practices go back into effect.[42]

Chapter Two

A Proposed Rationale for the Mourning Legislation

A brief summation of post-biblical mourning practices and requirements has been presented until this point. Nowhere does this legislation set out to invest these practices with any specific rationale, nor do the Talmudic rabbis express any overarching purpose that would provide the unifying link for these apparently discrete mourning observances.

Certainly it would be a distortion to ascribe to rabbinic mourning practices the motives which some early anthropologists attributed to primitive mourning rites. We have already noted that Frazer and others injected a heavy apotropaeic dosage into primitive mourning rites. For these scholars, the rites were fundamentally taboos designed to protect the living from the feared dead. Garments were rent and sandals removed in order to prevent the dead from attaching themselves to the clothes of the living. One sat on the ground and hid his face in order to confuse the returning spirit of the dead. Ashes were thrown on the face and hair was allowed to grow long in an effort to make the mourner unrecognizable to these dreaded spirits.[43] Fortunately, some of the more recent anthropologists give fuller credit to primitive man's subtle insights into the elementals of death and

life, and to his ability to express, in a profound and poetic manner, the ambivalent and contradictory human response to death.[44]

In any case, we have seen that biblical and rabbinic Judaism
had little patience with cults of the dead, with ancestor worship,
or with rituals designed to appease the "evil" spirits of the dead.
In searching for a rationale for the Judaic mourning rites, it
should be understood initially that these rites are much more
than a series of disjointed and unrelated practices whose common core is fear. Furthermore, we should go beyond the psy-
chological-utilitarian motifs which claim that the mourning
rites are expressions of grief which should not be repressed, or
that the rites are important aids in overcoming grief,[45] or that
they are a necessary means for restoring the cohesion of the
group which has been profoundly shaken by death.[46]

The mourning laws are all these—but they are much more:
they express the life view of Israel. They are a reflection of the
classic Judaic view of man's relationship to himself and God,
and to death and *tum'ah*. In a word, the *halakhah* of mourning
illustrates in practice what the concept of *tum'ah* illustrates in
theory: that death desacralizes man and separates him from the
Divine, temporarily removing him from an intimate relationship
with God, with other men, and with himself.

The Mourner as a Depersonalized Being

How should a mourner react to the fact of death? He has now
experienced the death of a close blood relative. He has felt
acutely the effects of the termination of life and has seen the
incursion of *tum'ah* into the realm of what was once normative
living. He has observed at close proximity the ultimate opposite
of life. He has been brushed by the powerful non-life, non-active,
non-divine force which is *tum'ah*. Having known and experienced
the absence of life and sanctity, he is now required by law to
crystallize this cognition into concrete observances.

The law has the effect of making the mourner behave as if he himself were dead. He is now an incomplete person, and his daily life begins to reflect the fact of his incompleteness. His physical appearance and his body are neglected. His relationship with God is interrupted. He has no commonality or community with other men; the qualities and characteristics of a living human being are suspended. According to the Midrash, death is one of the aspects of human life which likens man to a beast.[47] In death, man has witnessed the ultimate opposite of life, of God, and of man, and he cannot now summarily leave death behind him and return quickly and easily into the land of the living. He knows now what it is to be without the breath of the God of life, and he can return to normal life and to renewed contact with the sacred only by degrees. In a word, the mourner must now live as an alien between the two worlds of life and death, moving towards sanctity and life.[48]

A careful examination of the specifics of Israelite mourning legislation indicates that the law would have the mourner react and behave in a manner not inconsistent with that *tum'ah* force he has just encountered. He has been touched by the anti-life aspects of *tum'ah* and he himself therefore becomes less lifelike, less complete as a being. His brush with death and *tum'ah* causes him, at least for the moment, to lose his identity as a person and as a human. For just as *tum'ah* separates man from God, it also separates man from the fraternity and community of other men, and separates man from his essential self, from his essence as a person. In the face of the Ultimate Category of *tum'ah*, the human being ceases to exist as a person. We have seen that God and *tum'ah* do not reside together. Similarly, man as a person, as an identity, as a being, as a living creature, and as the image of God, cannot be present together with *tum'ah*. It has already been suggested (p. 24) that *tum'ah* represents the desacralizing qualities of death. *Tum'ah* desacralizes all of life.

It removes from life those very qualities that differentiate life from death. The mourning rites are a physical expression—in the conduct of the mourner—of this desacralization, which is in this case a devitalizing, a depersonalizing, a deidentifying of the mourner in his normal relationships and connections.[49]

Therefore, he who has been involved with death and *tum'ah* refrains from participating in those aspects of life that express a relationship with God, or his fellow man, or himself.

His essence as a person has been diminished and he does not cut his hair, for the cutting of hair is a sign of a man's concern with his person. Thus, the Rabbis declare that an Israelite king was required to cut his hair daily in order to maintain his dignity.[50] The mourner allows his hair to grow untended and uncared for: there is no concern now with his physical being.

For the same reason, he allows his garments to become unclean. And, at the moments of death and burial, he rends the garment he is wearing—and wears the rent garment during the mourning period. Garments and man's concern with them are manifestations of the fully living. For example, it is said of R. Johanan that he referred to his clothes as "my dignifiers."[51] That is, clothing dignifies and honors the wearer. As one who is now temporarily stripped of the dignity and honor of being a person, the mourner rends the symbol of this dignity. Further, as a manifestation of his status as a nonperson, he does not anoint or wash himself.

His being as a person has been reduced, his identity as an individual has melted away, and he has no marital relations— which has a potential of creating a new life and a new identity; nor may he take a new wife.

His essence as a man has been decreased and he walks barefoot in common with the beasts. Shabbat 152a reports that a Sadducee once saw R. Joshua without shoes and said, "One who is dead is better off than one who goes without shoes."[52]

He has been depersonalized, and he may not engage in work,[53] since work sustains his life and is a manifestation of his person and of his connection with himself and with others.

He has been touched by desacralizing death and *tum'ah,* and he may not study Torah which is called *Torath ḥayim*—"the Torah of life"—Proverbs 3:2; 3:18; 4:22; 9:11—and which is an aspect of God and which connects man with Him and His sacredness.[54]

He has a diminished identity as a person and he does not sit, in the accepted mode of persons, on a chair or couch. He sits on the ground in a configuration of lowness and diminution.

The same consideration causes him to refrain from sleeping in the normal mode: He "overturns the couch," and as we have noted above (p. 86), the reason for this is the concept of *demut diyuqni natati bakhem*—"my image have I implanted in you." [55] The image of God within man has been affected by death. That is to say, once again, that death and *tum'ah* have "de-imagized" man who was created in the Image. By virtue of his contact with death and *tum'ah,* the *demut diyuqni*—"the form of my image"—that which makes the essential man, has been diminished. Overturning or inverting the bed during the mourning period is a symbol of this depersonalization. "Turn over the middle-man (the bed on which life is conceived)," says the Talmud.[56]

For a similar reason, he does not prepare his own first meal following the burial. He has no relationship to himself, and at least at this one moment he symbolically possesses no food. Only a fully living person prepares his own food. He may, if he desires, fast; if he wishes to eat, the food must be prepared by others. And the menu must include foods which remind him of the "nonperson" condition in which he finds himself.[57]

Further depersonalization takes place. The head and face

are covered. The mourner says, in effect, I do not exist; I am not I; I am an alien in the land of the living.

Because he is not "I" he may not offer greetings—*sh'elat shalom* (literally, "asking of peace")—to his fellowman, nor may others offer greetings to him. He remains silent. Only a person, only an identity, can greet and be greeted in return. And *shalom*—the traditional greeting—is a symbol of community and fraternity.[58] It is significant that *shalom* is also considered to be one of the appellations of the deity, according to Shabbat 10b: "*Shalom* is the name of the Holy One, Blessed be He." [59] According to some opinions, greeting a mourner is permitted as long as the word "*shalom*" is not mentioned in the context of "peace unto you." [60] According to these opinions, at least, the desacralizing aspects of death and mourning are now clearly manifested; not only is *shalom* avoided because of its connotations of peace, perfection, community, and fraternity— of which the mourner is a direct opposite; *shalom* is avoided because of its additional connotations of the sacred, from which the mourner is now estranged.

In sum, the mourner is a diminished person, one who has been touched by the antilife of *tum'ah,* and he sits in rent garments, on the ground, without shoes, unkempt, unwashed; he engages neither in work nor in study of Torah; his head and face are covered, he greets and recognizes no one and, in turn, is greeted and recognized by no one.[61] And since he has experienced the desacralizing force of *tum'ah,* the *mourner may not offer up a sacrifice* for seven days. Nor, as we have seen, may he—at the initial moments of the presence of death—perform the positive precepts of prayer or phylacteries or the recitation of *amen.*[62]

Only during one day of the seven-day mourning period does the mourner return to a semblance of his former status as a man —and that is on the Sabbath day.[63] On this day his essence as a person is restored to him: on this one day he wears his shoes, extends and receives greetings, wears an untorn garment, straightens his couch (although he still may not engage in marital relations), and sits on an upright chair. No condolences may be offered him on the Sabbath. At the termination of the Sabbath, however, he reverts back to the normative status of mourning.

Characteristically, no reasons are given for the fact that the Sabbath supersedes mourning. Perhaps it is because the institution of the Sabbath in biblical and rabbinic tradition is a reminder that God is the Creator of the universe and of life. "For in six days the Lord made heaven and earth . . . and rested on the seventh day" (Exodus 20:11) is taken by the tradition to imply that he who observes the Sabbath day is stating, in effect, that God created the universe, while he who does not observe is, in effect, denying this.[64] In like manner, the Sabbath is considered to be a prefigure of the world-to-come. "The Sabbath is an example of the world-to-come," God said to Israel when He gave them the commandments.[65] "The Sabbath possesses a holiness like that of the world-to-come," say the Rabbis, and "the time to come is the day which will be a complete Sabbath and rest in life eternal." [66]

It is perhaps because of the heavy emphasis of the Sabbath on life as created and on life as eternal, as well as on sanctity,[67] that there is a suspension of the nonlife, nonsacred regimen of the mourner.[68]

Silence in Mourning

The concept of silence during the mourning period is vital to the idea of mourning. Ezekiel 24:17, a key passage in rabbinic mourning legislation, states: "sigh in silence (*dom*)." There are a number of other instances of the root *dmm* in connection with mourning or lamenting.

a. Leviticus 10:3: ". . . and Aaron was silent (*vayidom*).
b. Isaiah 23:2: "Be silent (*domu*) inhabitants of the coast-land."
c. Psalms 4:5: "Commune with your heart upon your beds and be silent.
d. Psalms 30:13: "So that my glory may sing praise onto Thee and not be silent (*yidom*)"
e. Psalms 94:17: ". . . my soul had dwelt in silence (*dumah*) of death." (Note that the LXX renders this as ʼἅδγ, Hades.ʼ)
f. Lamentations 2:10: "The elders of the daughters of Zion sit upon the ground, they keep silence (*yidmu*)."
g. Lamentations 3:28: "That he sit in solitude and be silent (*veyidom*)." [69]

Significantly, it has been pointed out that the Accadian and Ugaritic cognates of *dmm* mean "to mourn, moan." [70] Elsewhere, Dahood supports this suggestion by reference to the earlier studies of Delitzsch in 1884 and Paul Haupt in 1909, both of whom showed the similarity between the Hebrew *dmm* and the Accadian *damamu as* "moan." [71] In the light of this evidence Dahood suggests that the biblical *dmm* passages cited above be translated not as "silent," but as "mourn, or moan." "Silence," writes Dahood, "seems to have played very little part in mourning ceremonies." [72]

While it is not unacceptable to translate *dmm* as "mourn," one must take issue with Dahood's statement concerning the role of silence in mourning. It is quite clear from the rabbinic texts cited above that silence is indeed an integral part of mourning rites. The prohibition against the mourner's asking after anyone's well-being—the need for him to be silent in his mourning—is supported by rabbinic reference to Ezekiel 24:17, "sigh in silence" (*dom*). This would indicate that, to the Rabbis, silence was not identical or synonymous with mourning, that it was not simply another word for mourning but was rather a significant and necessary means of expressing one's mourning. By the act of silence, by refraining from ordinary and unnecessary talk, the mourner expresses in silence the new status which is his as the result of his contact with death and *tum'ah*. The silence of the mourner, in fact, manifests most eloquently that element of the depersonalization of the mourner and his radical separation from man, from God, and from himself which is the overriding condition of the death and *tum'ah* experience. As Job 2:13 puts it, "And no one spoke a word to him." And it is significant that the reason lentils are among the foods served at the funeral meal is: ". . . as the lentil has no mouth, so is the mourner." [73]

Silence, then, far from playing "very little part in mourning ceremonies," is fully consistent with the Talmudic idea of mourning. And in the *dmm* passages in Isaiah, Psalms and Lamentations it is silence in its literal sense which is conveyed by *dmm*—the kind of silence which is associated with lamenting and mourning.

Patterns of Paradox in the Halakhah of Mourning

The laws of mourning which we have just examined contain within them a polarity and a "pattern of paradox" quite similar in kind to those already noted in the first chapter, where the curious symbiotic relationship between sanctity and defilement was discussed.[74] In this section we will examine some of the paradoxes within the mourning legislation.

The words *ḥag* and *ebel*—"feast" and "mourning"—in Amos 8:10 ("and I will turn your feasts into mourning") are very significant. The fact that Amos juxtaposes *ḥag* and *ebel* in one passage is the key support for the establishment of the seven-day mourning period, as we have seen in the discussion on mourning.[75]

In a custom reminiscent of this curious combining of *ḥag* and *ebel,* both Syrian weddings and funerals "are still celebrated on the level surface of threshing floors." [76] Genesis 50:10 refers to Atad's threshing floor at Jacob's mourning ceremony.[77]

The juxtaposition of death and marriage is not uncommon. There are attestations in many cultures of a) bridal couples decorating the graves of their relatives; b) a mass for the dead recited at weddings; c) a procession to the cemetery after the wedding breakfast; d) brides married in widow's mourning habit; e) shrouds and coffin boards made at the time of the wedding.[78] Van der Leeuw explains all this by noting that "in sacred life every crisis is one of death." [79] Therefore, man attempts to invest the ultimate and fearful moments of life's crises and transition periods—birth, marriage, death—with some control and some contact with the Divine.

This paradoxical combining of feasting and lamenting, of wedding and funeral, is further manifested in several rabbinic instances.

a) J. Ketubot 1, 1, states, "Just as one comforts the mourner for seven days in mourning, so also does one make the couple joyous for seven days at a wedding feast."

b) Semaḥot 6:3: "On the first day of mourning, the mourner may not wear his phylacteries." Succah 25b, Moed Qatan 21a, and J. Moed Qatan 3, 5 record similar mourning restrictions concerning phylacteries. One of the reasons for this is that phylacteries signify joy.[80] It is noteworthy, however, that even on those days of the mourning period during which the mourner is permitted to wear his phylacteries, he must, according to the same Mishnah, "remove them at any time during the seven-day mourning period that others come to comfort him." [81]

Zlotnick suggests that the mourner removes his phylacteries at the appearance of new comforters (i.e., those who have not as yet comforted him,) in order to show that his earlier intense grief is still strong. This, he suggests, is similar to the practice at wedding feasts. Such feasts continue for the first week of marriage, "but only for . . . 'a new face,' that is, when one who has not heard the blessing arrives." Each of the wedding feasts during the first seven days requires at least one new guest who has not been present previously. In effect, the arrival of a "new face" during both the mourning and wedding periods affects their respective rites.[82]

c) Rabbinical tradition states that Solomon built two gates in the Temple: one for bridegrooms, and one for mourners and excommunicants. Jerusalemites would gather between these two gates on the Sabbath and would offer condolences to the mourners and excommunicants on one side, and offer good wishes to the brides and grooms on the other.[83] We will note the significance of this material during the discussion of the mourner as excommunicant; it is also significant here, since it hints at a common element in feasting (bridegrooms) and lamenting (mourner and excommunicant).

d) The Talmud teaches that "one interrupts the study of the Torah for the leading out of the dead [a funeral], and for the bringing in of a bride [a wedding]." [84]

e) Certain foods are common to feasting and mourning. The lentil, according to Midrash Rabbah, "has in it mourning and has in it feasting," while Midrash Tanḥuma states that lentils used to be brought both to the house of mourning and to the house of feasting. We also find that wine, always associated with feasting and gladness, was created, according to one opinion, "for the purpose of comforting mourners," and was utilized for mourners in rabbinic times.[85]

The rabbinic exegesis of the "feast" and "mourning" of Amos 8:10 is, then, not merely a capricious or arbitrary reading of the text. The connections between feasting and mourning are repeatedly mirrored in the ancient world and in rabbinic sources.

In addition to the paradoxes of marriage and death, there are similar polarities between birth and death, and between the priest and death. The joy of birth and the sadness of death are inextricably linked in the Midrash. It points out that a father is joyous at the birth of a son, although he knows full well that the son will ultimately die. Nevertheless, "at the time of joy, joy; at the time of mourning, mourning." [86] This Midrash is echoed in a cryptic commentary of R. Jacob b. Asher on Leviticus 12:2: ". . . a woman who gives birth to a male shall be *tamé* for seven days. . . ." R. Jacob b. Asher (14th century) comments, *ad loc.*: "In the manner that he comes, so does he go." That is to say, just as a man's birth results in *tum'ah* for the mother for seven days, so does his death result in mourning for seven days.

An additional paradox is found in the restrictions on marital relations during mourning, and upon approaching sanctity. As we have already noted, a mourner is forbidden to engage in marital relations during the first week of mourning.[87] Sexual abstinence, however, is not limited to the experience of profane death. It is also required in order to approach the sacred. In I Samuel 21:5, holy bread is offered to David on condition that "the young men have kept themselves from women"; in Exodus 19:15, at the Sinaitic revelation, Israel is commanded, "do not approach a woman"; Moses separates completely from his wife because the presence of God (*shekhinah*) descends upon him without notice.[88] Basing itself on the same passage in Exodus, one rabbinic opinion holds that he who has seminal emissions may not even hear "words of Scripture." [89]

In effect, then, contact with the two ultimate opposites—on the one hand, the sacred; on the other, death—each involves sexual abstinence. In the former, sexual abstinence makes possible the ensuing contact with the sacred; in the latter, the abstinence is a result of the experience of death.

A similar relationship is evident between the Nazarite, whose contact with the sacred restricts him from cutting his hair for thirty days, and the mourner, whose contact with death and defilement also restricts him from cutting his hair for thirty days.

Perhaps most paradoxical of all is the very method by which the laws of mourning are derived from biblical passages. Almost every normative mourning practice is negatively derived from a biblical priestly obsevance. Thus Moed Qatan 14b:

> A mourner is forbidden to cut his hair, since the Divine Law ordained the sons of Aaron, "Let not the hair of your heads grow long" (Leviticus 10:6), we infer that for everyone else, cutting the hair is forbidden.

Similarly, the mourner must, "muffle his head" (i.e., cover almost his entire face) because Ezekiel, who was a priest, was told *not* to muffle his head (Ezekiel 24:17; Moed Qatan 15a). Whether it be restrictions on the mourner concerning phylacteries, or offering normal greetings, or studying Scripture, or washing his clothes, or rending his garments, they are all inversely derived from priests.[90]

The paradox is this: the very practices concerning death and mourning are based on the priests, for whom there are so many restrictions concerning death and mourning. *There is no open and clear biblical mourning legislation directed to non-priests.* What the priest is forbidden to practice in his mourning—because he *is* a priest—the Israelite must practice in his mourning—because he is *not* a priest. Only the fact of his priestly sanctity prevents the priest from observing mourning rites in the normative way. Perhaps here, too, there is a further hint of the strict quarantine which must be maintained between the priest and death. This may adumbrate, however dimly, the idea that the Living God does not speak directly of death and mourning. At the moment that God speaks to man, death does not exist and is not possible. If it must be discussed, if there must be mourning legislation, it is done obliquely, within a framework of sanctity and priesthood.

All this is an additional thread in that striking pattern of opposites we noted earlier vis-à-vis defilement and sanctity: those very elements which are most diametrically opposed frequently stand in some close relationship to one another, as if they were a manifestation of man's contradictory and ambivalent response to death.[91]

Mourner and Excommunicant: Two Types of Separation from God

We have seen that in many of his requirements a mourner is a symbolic representation of someone who is now remote and separated from God. Some support for this view can be derived from the legislation dealing with excommunication, or *nidui*.

The purpose of excommunication is clear and self-evident: it is designed to isolate and exclude the excommunicant from intimate association with God and God's society. Thus, only his immediate family may associate with him, sit within his four cubits, or eat with him.[92] The other forms and practices through which rabbinic law effects the isolation of the excommunicant are therefore of great importance.

It is significant that rabbinic law implements the isolation of the excommunicant by applying to him almost every law of the mourner. In effect, the law is apparently saying that when it is necessary to exclude a man from God and God's society, there is no more appropriate expression of this exclusion than those forms already practiced by the mourner.

The primary source for our suggestion that the excommunicant and the mourner have much in common is in Moed Qatan 14b ff. In these folios, the Talmud specifically compares the duties of the excommunicant to those of the mourner and finds them identical in almost every way.

Like the mourner, the excommunicant—

a) may not cut his hair;
b) muffles his head;
c) may not greet others or be greeted;
d) may not teach or study Scripture in public; [93]
e) may not wash his clothes;
f) may not wear shoes or sandals;
g) may not offer sacrifices in the Temple;
h) rends his clothes. [94]

The Talmud questions, but comes to no definite conclusion, as to whether the following restrictions, which are part of the mourner's regimen, are also in effect when one is an excommunicant:

a) prohibition against wearing phylacteries;
b) requirement to "overturn the couch";
c) prohibition against marital intercourse ("use of the conjugal bed").

In addition, it was customary for the excommunicant to wear mourning clothes [95] and, like the mourner, his period of excommunication lasted seven days in Babylonia. (In Palestine, it lasted for thirty days [Moed Qatan 17a], which is also an established mourning period.) [96]

As already noted,[97] early rabbinic sources reveal that Solomon built two gates in his Temple, one for bridegrooms and one for excommunicants and mourners. The people would assemble between these two gates and offer condolences (literally, *hesed*) at one gate to the mourners and excommunicants, and good wishes at the other gate to the newly married couples.[98]

Mishnah Middot 2:2 renders a similar picture. All who entered the Temple Mount would enter on the right side and leave by the left.[99] Among those who entered at the left were "one to whom something untoward had happened." The Mishnah gives two examples of those who must enter at the left: one is a mourner; the second is an excommunicant.[100]

A remarkable similarity between the mourner and the excommunicant is evident here. The mourner, of course, becomes subject to the mourner's restrictions through no trespass of his own, but because of someone else's death. But having experienced, however unwillingly, death's defilement, he must now separate himself from God's sanctity for a certain period of time. Conversely, the excommunicant, by his own acts, has deliberately removed himself from the province of the sacred, and is punished by having God's ban placed upon him for a certain period of time. Put another way, God excludes himself from the mourner, while the excommunicant excludes himself from God. Whatever the ultimate cause, however, exclusion is the common element of both, and the fact that the restrictions upon the mourner and upon the excommunicant are so interwoven supports the thesis that *the mourner is a symbolic excommunicant,* and that the mourner's restrictions are an attempt to exclude death and its associates from intimate association with God.

"Mocking the Poor": The Dead as Desacralized

Further support for the concept of the dead as estranged and desacralized is found in the rabbinic principle of *lo'eg larash*— "mocking the poor"—which is a primary manifestation of the profound rabbinic concern for the welfare of the dead.

The principle of *lo'eg larash* is based on Proverbs 17:5: 'he that mocks the poor blasphemes his Maker." The "poor," according to rabbinic interpretation, refers not only to the physically and materially poor, but to the spiritually poor as well. That is to say, it refers to the dead, who are considered "poor" since they are now unable to perform the biblical precepts.[101]

> A man should not walk in a cemetery with phylacteries on his head or a Scroll of Law in his arm, and recite the *Shma'* prayer, and if he does so he comes under the heading of "He that mocks the poor." [102]

For the living to perform any divine precept in the presence of the dead is to mock the dead and to insult them. The Talmud relates that two sages were once walking about in a cemetery, and the biblically prescribed fringe (Numbers 15:38) of one was trailing on the ground. His companion said to him, "Lift it up, so that they [the dead] should not say, 'Tomorrow they are coming to join us and now they are insulting us.'" Similarly, one may not discuss "words of Scripture" in the presence of the dead,[103] nor may one inquire about a religious law while in the presence of a bier.[104]

This principle of "mocking the dead" thus is another indication that the dead are totally removed from the cult of God. Shabbat 30a states that when a man dies he is "restrained from Torah and good deeds." The dead are "poor" because in their present state they are unable to serve Him.

Chapter Three

The Rabbinic Lament: Estrangement and Desacralization

One further area remains for us to explore in this discussion of death and defilement as estrangement and desacralization: that of the rabbinic funeral song, or lament. In certain of their characteristics, the rabbinic laments are a literary manifestation of death as estrangement.

While research on biblical laments and funeral songs is profuse, varied and abundant,[105] the study of rabbinic laments and funeral songs has been almost totally neglected. This is in keeping with the general spirit of Western scholarship which has tended to overlook the rabbinic tradition. Nevertheless, the study of these post-biblical laments provides an important counterpoint to those in the Bible.

The Talmud records the words of some twenty-nine funeral songs. Many of these are found in Moed Qatan 25b ff., while the others are scattered throughout the Talmud. These laments have been brought together in the following collection, which contains the full Hebrew and Aramaic texts of the laments together with English translations.[106]

I

Lament recited when Hillel died:

Alas, the pious man,	הי חסיד
alas, the humble man,	הי עניו
the disciple of Ezra	תלמידו של עזרא

—Sanhedrin 11a

II

Recited by R. Gamaliel and R. Eleazar at the death of Samuel the Little, who was childless:

Over him it is well to weep.	על זה נאה לבכות
Over him it is well to mourn.	על זה נאה להתאבל
When kings die,	כשמלכים מתים
they leave their crowns	
to their children.	מניחים כתריהם לבניהם
The rich die,	עשירים מתים
they leave their wealth	
to their children.	מניחים עושרם לבניהם
Samuel the Little took the world's	שמואל הקטן נטל חמודות
treasures **and went his way.**	של עולם והלך לו

—Semaḥot (Ebel Rabbati) 8.7

III

When Samuel the Little died:

Alas, the pious man,	הי חסיד
alas, the humble man,	הי עניו
the disciple of Hillel.	תלמידו של הלל

—Sanhedrin 11a

IV

Eulogy suggested for the man who prays properly:

Alas, the humble man,	אי עניו
Alas, the pious man,	אי חסיד
One of the disciples of	
our Father Abraham.	מתלמידיו של אברהם אבינו

—*Berakhot 6b* (E.F.)

V

Lament sung by R. Akiba upon the death of R. Eliezer:

My father, my father,	אבי אבי
the chariot of Israel	רכב ישראל ופרשיו
and its horseman.	הרבה מעות יש לי
I have many coins	
but no money changer	ואין לי שלחני להרצותן
to accept them.[107]	

—*Sanhedrin 68a* (E.F.)

VI

On the death of Rabbi, Bar-Kappara tore his cloak and reported the death to the Rabbis thus:

The Angels and the just	אראלים ומצוקים אחזו בארון
have taken hold of the Holy Ark,[108]	נצחו אראלים את המצוקים
The Angels overpowered the just,	
And the Holy Ark	ונשבה ארון הקדש
has been captured.	

—*Ketubot 104a.*

VII

Rab said, The women of Shokhen-Zeb say:

Woe for the departed   ויי לאזלא
Woe for the loss.[109]   ויי לחבילא

—*Moed Qatan 28b* (E.F.)

VIII

Withdraw the bone from the tooth [110]   גוד גרמא מככא
and let water be put into the kettles.[111] ונמטי מיא לאנטיכי

—*Ibid.* (E.F.)

IX

Be muffled and cover yourselves,   עטוף וכסו טורי
   O mountain peaks,
for he is of high lineage   דבר רמי ובר רברבי הוא
   and great ancestry.

—*ibid.* (E.F.)

X

Borrow a Milesian robe [112]   שייול איצטלא דמילתא
For a free man[113]   לבר חורין דשלימו זוודיה
   who left no provision.

—*Ibid.* (E.F.)

XI

Comes hurrying and scurrying   רהיט ונפל אמעברא
   aboard the ferry,   ויזופתא יזיף
and having to borrow his fare.

—*Ibid.*

XII

Our brothers are merchants
who are tested
by the goods they sell.

אחנא תגרי

אזבוגי מבדקו

—Ibid.

XIII

This death or that death,
our bruises are the rate of interest.

מותא כי מותא
ומרעין חיבוליא

—Ibid.

XIV

On the day when Abraham our Father passed away from the
world, all the great ones of the nations of the world stood in a
line and said:

Woe to the world that has lost
   its leader,
and woe to the ship that has
   lost its pilot

אוי לו לעולם שאבד מנהיגו

ואוי לה לספינה שאבד קברניטא.

—Baba Bathra 91a-b

XV

Lament on the occasion of a flood:

More than a third have disappeared
   in the water,
remember and have mercy.
We have strayed from Thee
as a woman from her husband,
Cast us not off as a sign
   of the bitter waters.[114]

באו רוב שלישית במים
זכור ורחם
תעינו מאחריך
כאשה מבעלה

אל תזניחנו כאות מי מרה.

—Moed Qatan 25b

XVI

A certain child opened his funeral oration for Rabbah b. R. Huna thus:

A scion of ancient stock came up from Babylon,	גזע ישישים עלה מבבל
with records of prowess in scholarly battles,	ועמו ספר מלחמות
Twice numerous pelican and bittern from far,	קאת וקפוד הוכפלו לראות
Came from the ravage and ruin in Shin'ar [Babylon].	בשוד ושבר הבא משנער
When he views his world with displeasure,	קצף על עולמו
he seizes souls in exacting measure,	וחמס ממנו נפשות
awaiting their coming as new brides with delight.	ושמח בהם ככלה חדשה
The Rider of Clouds is joyous and glad	רוכב ערבות שש ושמח
when a pure and righteous soul approaches him.	בבא אליו נפש נקי וצדיק

—*Ibid.* (partial trans. by E.F.)

XVII

Lament for a father named Ḥonin who died on the day his child was born:

Joy to sorrow is turned	שמחה לתוגה נהפכה
Gladness and sadness are one.	ששון ויגון נדבקו
At the time of joy he sighed	בעת שמחתו נאנח
At the time of the gracious [infant]	בעת חנינתו
the gracious [father] was lost	אבד חנינו

—*Ibid.*

XVIII

Rabbah b. Naḥmani died uttering the words, "tahor, tahor". ("pure, pure"). He was the pre-eminent authority on purity and impurity. A Heavenly Voice cried out:

Happy art thou,   אשריך רבה בר נחמני
   Rabbah b. Naḥmani,   שגופך טהור
for thy body is pure,
and thy soul   ויצאתה נשמתך בטהור
   has departed with "pure."

                  —*Baba Meẓia 86a* (E.F.)

XIX

A man (an idolator) once went about saying:

Alas for the valiant rider   ווי לפרשא זריזא
Who was in Pumpeditha and died.[116]   דהוה בפומפדיתא ושכיב
           —*Yebamot 121b* (E.F.)

XX

Rava said, When a man dies in Babylon, they mourn for him in Tiberias, saying:

Great was he in Sheshakh‌ [Babylon] [117]   גדול הוא בששך
and he has a name in Rakath.[118]   ושם לו ברקת

                —*Megillah 6a*

XXI

And when the coffin is taken there, they mourn for him thus:

Ye lovers of the remnants,[119]   אוהבי שרידים
   dwellers in Rakath,   יושבי רקת
   go forth and receive   צאו וקבלו
   the slaughtered of the depths.[120]   הרוגי עומק

                —*Ibid.*

XXII

When R. Zera departed, a certain mourner opened his dirge:

The land of Shin'ar conceived and bore him,	ארץ שנער הרה וילדה
the land of beauty [Palestine] raised its precious one,	ארץ צבי גידלה שעשועיה
Woe to her, says Rakath,	אוי נא לה אמרה רקת
for she has lost her precious vessel.	כי אבדה כלי חמדתה

—Ibid.

XXIII

Alas O lion	הוי ארי
Alas O mighty one.[121]	הוי גבור

—Semaḥot 1:9

XXIV

Alas O faithful witness	הוי עד נאמן
who ate the fruit of his own labor.[122]	אוכל בעמלו

—Ibid.

XXV

Lament for two sons and a daughter:

Woe, woe,	הוי הוי
Bridegrooms and bride.	חתנים וכלה

—Semaḥot 11:4

XXVI

Alas, misguided fool	הוי נשלה
Alas, misguided fool. [123]	הוי נשלה

—Ibid.

XXVII

The opening of a funeral oration for Rabina, by a professional eulogizer:

Ye palms, sway your heads
for him who was righteous
    as a palm.[124]
Let us lament by night as by day
for him who meditated by night as
    by day.

תמרים הניעו ראש

על צדיק כתמר

נשים לילות כימים

על משים לילות כימים

—Moed Qatan 25b (E.F.)

XXVIII

A noted funeral orator, Bar-Kipok, suggested this funeral oration for R. Ashi:

If a flame falls among the cedars,
what shall lowly hyssops of the
    wall do?
If Leviathan is hauled up
    by a hook,
what shall the fishes of a stream do?
If a hook falls in a rushing stream,
what shall marshy ponds do?

אם בארזים נפלה שלהבת

מה יעשו איזובי קיר

לויתן בחכה הועלה
מה יעשו דגי רקק
בנחל שוטף נפלה חכה
מה יעשו מי גבים

—Ibid. (E.F.)

XXIX

Another noted lamenter, Bar Abin, objected to the use of "hook" or "flame." He suggested this oration:

Weep for the mourners	בכו לאבילים
and not for what is lost.	ולא לאבידה
For she has gone to rest,	שהיא למנוחה
and we are gone to grief.	ואנו לאנחה

—*Ibid.* (E.F.) (R. Ashi objected to both versions because of the metaphors "flame" and "lost.")

Similarities Between Biblical and Rabbinic Laments

The rabbinic laments have certain features which are characteristic of biblical laments. The "woe-call" of the Bible—*hoi* and *'oi*—(I Kings 13:30; Jeremiah 22:18, 34:5; Amos 5:16; Ezekiel 30:2; Isaiah 4:7, and many other instances)—is echoed post-biblically as well.[125] A total of eleven funeral songs of the twenty-nine studied contain some form of the woe-call. These are Laments XXII, VII, XXIII, XXIV, XXVI, XXV, IV, I, III, XIV, XVI.[126]

Another feature of the biblical lament is the emphasis on the past history of the deceased. The *qinnah* in Ezekiel 19:2-10, for example, refers to Israel's early history. Several of the Talmudic laments make similar references.

Great was he in Sheshakh
And he has a name in Rakath.

—*Lament XX*

When R. Zera departed, a certain mourner began his dirge:

The land of Shin'ar conceived and bore him.
The land of beauty raised its precious one.

—*Lament XXII*

When Rabbah b. R. Huna died, a certain child began his funerary oration thus:

> A scion of ancient stock
> came up from Babylon. . . .
>   —*Lament XVI*

The abandonment and hopelessness of the survivors is a typical sentiment in biblical laments. While this quality is not characteristic of rabbinic laments, there are three examples of it. Lament XXIX cries:

> Weep for the mourners
> and not for what is lost,
> For she has gone to rest
> And we are gone to grief.

R. Akiba, in Lament V, complains that now that R. Eliezer is gone, there is no one to whom he can bring his religious and legal questions. And when Abraham our Father passed away, all the great ones of the world said:

> Woe to the world that has lost its leader
> And woe to the ship that has lost its pilot
>   —*Lament XIV*

Jahnow refers to "das Schema Einst und Jetzt" (the Then and the Now) as characteristics of biblical laments. A stark contrast is drawn between the glory that once was and the tragedy that now is. This scheme is found only rarely in rabbinic laments. There are several Midrashic and Talmudic one-line eulogies which contain a hint of this. See Qiddushin 39b: "Shall the mouth that uttered pearls lick the dust?" Abot d'R. Nathan 38:31 is almost identical, as is the citation in Jelinek's *Bet Hamidrash,* V. 6, p. 23.

Unique Qualities of the Rabbinic Lament

While it is true that rabbinic laments assimilate certain features of biblical funeral songs and ignore others entirely, it should not be assumed that they have no unique characteristics of their own. They contain certain indigenous features from which a basic literary pattern is discernible.

For example, in characterizing the biblical lament, Jahnow's *Schema,* notes an emphasis on:

a) the bodily excellence and physical strength of the departed (II Samuel 1, 21 ff.); b) his beautiful garments, wives, children, (II Samuel 1:21 ff.), b) his beautiful garments, wives, children, wealth (Exodus 27:3 ff.; Lamentations 4:5); c) his weapons (II Samuel 1:21 ff.; Ezekiel 32:27).

unalterability and inevitability of death (Jeremiah 9:21; Amos 5:2; Ezekiel 19:9; 14); b) the mystery of death (II Samuel 3:33 f.); c) the type of death (II Samuel 3:33 f.: Lamentations 1:19 f.; 2:11, 21; 4:5) d) the joy of the enemy (II Samuel 1:20).

None of these features is present in the rabbinic laments of the Talmud. Only in one instance is bodily excellence alluded to:

Alas O lion, Alas O mighty one.
—*Lament XXIII*

It is noteworthy that even in this single example, the lament is directed toward a slave or a heathen. In Lament XIX, a certain dead Israelite is referred to as "the valiant rider," but the speaker here is himself an idolator.

When a funeral orator in rabbinic laments wishes to praise the past glories of an Israelite, he may refer to his noble family tree:

For he is of high lineage and great ancestry.
—*Lament IX*

Or to his good reputation:

> Great was he in Sheshakh
> and he has a name in Rakath.
> —*Lament XX*

Or to his righteousness:

> The Rider of the Clouds is joyous and glad
> When a pure and righteous soul approaches him.
> —*Lament XVI*

Or that he was pious, humble, and a scholar:

> Where is the pious man,
> Where is the humble man,
> One of the disciples of our Father Abraham?
> —*Laments I, III, IV*

Or that he was like the Holy Ark:

> ... The Holy Ark has been captured.
> —*Lament VI*

Or that he was pure:

> For thy body is pure
> And thy soul has departed with "pure."
> —*Lament XVIII*

It is evident, then, that references to bodily excellence or strength, such as are found in biblical laments, are absent from rabbinic laments.

This may reflect, of course, the respective *sitz im leben* of the two types of laments. The biblical lament is often recited for someone who has fallen in battle (II Samuel 1:21 ff.), or for someone who has been a great warrior (II Samuel 3:33 f.), with the concomitant stress on physical prowess. By contrast, many of the rabbinic laments are recited for sages. Hence the emphasis on humility, piety, scholarship, good lineage, personal sanctity.[127]

The different rabbinical *sitz* also accounts for the other dissimilarities. Rabbinic laments do not mention the weapons of the deceased nor the hateful joy of the enemy nor the type of death as do the biblical: obviously, these are irrelevant when one is lamenting a scholar. This also accounts for the entirely different mood and tone of the two types. The biblical laments are far more bitter, powerful, and passionate. The infamy and incomprehensibility of death is decried (II Samuel 3:33 f.). The suddenness of death, and the transitory nature of life's glory is mourned (II Samuel 1:19). There is, in biblical laments, a much more profound element of grief and despair and affliction.

That the rabbinic laments do not possess the sheer force and elemental power of their classical biblical counterparts is understandable. The biblical laments are usually uttered in a context of sudden death at the prime of life on the field of battle, and they involve destruction of massive proportions. In such an extraordinary context, the agonized cry of grief is far more intense and dramatic than that of an ordinary funeral—even if it be for a great leader. This also accounts for the *absence of consolation* in rabbinic laments, although it is present in biblical laments. Absence of consolation may also be due to the concept that consolation is not offered in a formal eulogy, as in Mishnah 'Abot 4:23: "Do not comfort your fellow when his dead lies before him."

The most salient feature of the rabbinic lament lies in its profane quality. Sentiments about the Divine are not articulated. There is one reference to angels, in Lament VI, but the deity is never mentioned by name—and in only one instance is the deity even alluded to: Lament XVI records the opening words of the funeral oration of "a certain child" who was eulogizing Rabbah b. R. Huna:

> When he views the world with displeasure,
> he seizes souls in exacting measure,
> rejoicing in them as with a new bride.
> The Rider of the Clouds is joyous and glad
> when a pure and righteous soul approaches him.

"He" and "Rider of the Clouds" are clear references to the Divine. (Lament XV is more of a prayer than a pure lament, and hence also bears an allusion to the deity.) In this element of profaneness, the rabbinic laments, of course, follow the pattern of the biblical laments.[128]

It should also be noted that rabbinic laments rarely mention the fact that the deceased actually died. In one of the Aramaic laments (XIII), the root *meth* is specifically uttered:

> *Mutha ki mutha*
> This death or that death.

In Lament XXI we find *haruge,* "the slaughtered." In II there are references to kings and rich men dying. But the clear and unequivocal statement that the deceased for whom the lament is sung actually died—this is missing. Even in II, which utilizes *met* in reference to kings and rich men, the dead Samuel, "went his way"—the lamenter studiously avoiding the use of *met*. In VI, Rabbi does not die. Rather, "the Holy Ark has been captured." In other laments, the euphemisms for death or dying are: "the soul departs" (XVIII), and "lost" (XIV, XVII, XXII,

XXIX). The use of "died" in XIX is a free translation of *shak-hib,* literally, "lay down."

That the refusal to mention death by name is more than a poetic nicety is indicated by the following: When Rabbi dies, Bar-Kappara reports the death to the Sages, using the euphemisms of the angels and the Holy Ark (Lament VI), whereupon they surmise that he has died. Bar-Kappara replies,

> "You said it, I did not say it." The Sages furthermore announced that whoever said Rabbi was dead (on the day he died) would be stabbed with a sword.[129]

A further characteristic of the rabbinic lament is the absence of ordinary proper names. The names of the deceased are rarely spoken, and countries are addressed not by their accepted names but by some recondite and oblique reference. Babylonia is "the depths," or "Shin'ar," or "Sheshakh" (XX, XXI); Tiberias is "Rakath" (XX); Israel is "lover of the remnants" and "the beauteous land' (XXI, XXII). In only one instance is Babylon called by the normative "Babel" (XVI). And in Lament XIX, the idolator laments for the "valiant rider" who died in the city of Pumpeditha.

In only two instances are the names of the deceased spoken. In II, Samuel the Little is named, and in XVIII, Rabbah b. Nahmani is named. (There is a word-play on Honin in XVII, but the actual name of the deceased is not used.)

The absence of proper names is quite different from the usage of biblical laments, which are hardly reticent in this regard. In David's lament in II Samuel 1:17-27, Saul and Jonathan are each mentioned four times. Among geographical references, we find Judah, Gilboa, Gath, Ashkelon, and the Philistines. In the lament of II Samuel 3:33 f, the name of the dead Abner is uttered, and Ezekiel's laments in 27:3 f., 28:12 f., and 32:2 ff., the object of the *qinah* is clearly named.

There is no ready explanation for the shunning of names in rabbinic laments. Perhaps it is nothing more than a poetic technique; perhaps it points to the formal and ritual aspects of the lament genre. Since it was not composed specifically for each occasion, there was evidently a conventional form used at every funeral, and the particular name of the departed was not an essential component of the song. By contrast, the extant biblical laments, while they contain many formalized qualities, are less contrived and are apparently tailored to the specific person or event at hand.

There are a number of rabbinic indicators which point to the existence of a formalized lament. Berakhot 6b records the eulogy suggested for a man who has "a fixed place for his prayer" (Lament IV). Sanhedrin 11a records the lament recited for Hillel, and is almost identical (I). And when Samuel the Little died, the same source records the lament, again in the same form (III). In each case, (I, III, IV), the lament begins with a woe-call, refers in the first two lines to the "pious man" and the "humble man," and concludes with the idea that the deceased lived according to the teachings of a great and noble forebear—Father Abraham, Ezra the Scribe, or Hillel.

The Talmud presents a remarkable substantiation for the existence of a formalized lament in rabbinic times:

> The Rabbis wished to use the same words of the lament which had been sung for Samuel the Little and for Hillel for R. Judah b. Baba (martyred in the Hadrianic persecution in the second century), but the troublous conditions of the times did not permit it, for no funeral orations were [permitted to be] delivered over those who were martyred by the [Roman] government.[130]

It is therefore quite possible that the consistent absence of the deceased's name in rabbinic laments is a manifestation of their ritually formalized nature.[131]

It should be noted that there is evidently universal significance attached to the names of the dead. Early mankind ascribed important sacral qualities to such names.[132] For example, the aborigine tribe of Abipones in South America avoids with horror one particular class of names: the names of the dead. When referring to the departed, they indulge in periphrasis: "the man who does not now exist." [133]

Among the Australian Wik Munkan aborigines, the mention of a name is forbidden for three years after the death of its bearer. Certain names of close relatives may never again be mentioned. Because of this taboo, they have developed a complex system of necronyms.[134] The Malagasy tribe of Madagascar observes a similar taboo against uttering the names of the deceased, and they are therefore given another name when they die.[135] This taboo, with certain variations, is also prevalent among the Australian Arunta,[136] while in New Guinea, if ordinary objects happen to have the same name as the dead, these words are dropped from the language.[137]

From the foregoing, then, it is evident that avoidance of the names of the dead are of considerable significance in a variety of cultures—and for a variety of reasons which are not always cross-cultural. The absence of names in rabbinic laments cannot be connected with fear of the dead. We have already noted [138] a remarkable absence of fear of the dead in biblical and rabbinic thought and practice. The best tentative conclusion is that the omission of names of the dead in rabbinic laments are a stylistic feature of this particular genre—a genre which, as noted above, manifests itself in several fixed and conventional forms.[139]

Literary Patterns in the Rabbinic Lament

A number of literary patterns are discernible in the rabbinic lament:

a) *Frequent allusions to biblical data and quotations of biblical phrases.* Akiba's lament (V) cites II Kings 2:12; *Sheshakh* in Lament XX is from Jeremiah 25:26; *Shin'ar* in XXII is from Genesis 14:1, while erez zvi of XXII is from Daniel 11: 16, 41; *havila* in VII echoes Psalms 18:5-6; *zadiq katamar* of XXVII is from Psalms 92; Lament XXVIII contains references to Leviticus 14:51-2; I Kings 5:13; Job 40:25; Jeremiah 14:3; Ezekiel 47:11. Lament XV has allusions to Habakkuk 3:2, Exodus 15:23-25, and the "trial by waters" of Numbers 5:2. These are but a few examples of the consistent references to the Bible in the rabbinic laments.

b) *Repetition of words and phrases.* Lament XXVII repeats *tamar* in the first two lines, and the phrase *lelot k'yamim* in the last two lines. It also repeats *nasim* and *mesim,* similar root words, in these two lines. In XXVIII, *mah ya'asu*—"What shall . . . do?" is a refrain repeated at the end of each couplet. II repeats *'al zeh, metim, menihin, livnehem.*

Lament VI provides an especially interesting example of consonantal repetition. Line 1 presents four major *aleph* sounds, and introduces one *zadi* sound. In line 2, two of the *aleph* sounds are repeated, and a new one is introduced: *eth.* At the same time, one *zadi* sound is repeated and a second *zadi* sound is introduced in *nizhu.* Of the twelve words in this lament, four are repeated twice: the last two words of line 3—*'aron haqodesh*—repeat the last two words of line 1. And *'arelim* and *mezuqim* of line 1 are both found again in line 2.

II, V, XVIII, XXVI, XXVII are further examples of the repetition of the last words in a line in order to form a more perfect identical rhyme.

c) *The doubling of the woe-call* is encountered in I, III, IV, V, VII, XXIII, XXV, XXVI.

d) Rabbinic laments are occasionally *paronomastic.* A play on words is seen in XVII, in which the lament for a man named

Ḥonin is climaxed by *b'eth ḥaninato 'abad ḥanino*. In XXIX, there is parallel word-play in each of its four lines: *abelim-abeda*; *menuḥah-anaḥah*. In XVIII, the last word, *tahor* has a dual meaning: it describes the state of purity in which the deceased died, and is also a direct quotation of his last words.

e) The images utilized by the laments are primarily of two types: those of nature, and of daily commerce. XXVII compares the deceased to a "palm." XXVIII refers to cedars, hyssop, fish, streams, and ponds. XVI refers to the pelican and bittern. Images of daily commerce are seen in XI: the deceased must "borrow his fare" for the "ferry"; in XII, merchants are "tested by the goods they sell"; XIII refers to interest rates; in V, R. Akiba, lamenting that there is no one now to answer his questions, cries, "I have many coins but no money changer to accept them." XIV refers to a ship's pilot. There are two instances of marriage images: Lament XVI compares the deity's joyful anticipation of the arrival of a pure soul to that of a groom awaiting the arrival of a "new bride"; and in the lament on the occasion of a flood (XV), Israel is said to have "strayed from Thee as a woman from her husband." Lament VI depicts a divine duel over the fate of a scholar who is compared to the Holy Ark which has been captured.

f) Several laments show evidence of specific poetic technique. Rhyme is evident in XVI. Lines 2, 3, and 6 end in the *'ot* sound, while line 5 ends with the *o* sound. Lament XXIX contains a rhyme in lines 3 and 4: *menuḥah* and *anaḥah*, which in turn form a weak rhyme to *'abedah* of line 2. The flood lament (XV) displays some alliteration, with each of its four lines ending with a word containing the *mem* sound. In addition, lines 3 and 4 are weakly rhymed. XVII also displays a weak rhyme in the last two words of each line.

g) Lament XVII provides a particularly instructive example of technique. Heavy alliteration is seen with the repetition of the *nun* sound in the last word of each line. In addition, there is a very subtle paralleling of sound in lines 1 and 2:

> *simḥa l'tuga nehephakhah*
> *sason v'yagon nidvku*

The consonant sounds in each of the first three words of line 1 are paralleled in the three words of line 2, as indicated. In the third word, the soft *peh* and *bet* are parallel, as are the guttural *kh* and *k*.

h) Rabbinic laments reveal no discernible metrical pattern or verse texture. The three unanswered questions of XXVIII possess a certain mournful tone. The eight brief words of XXIX are very carefully balanced, with the long vowels adding a heavy, doleful effect. Similar to this is the structure of XXVII, with its three words in the last line. A mournful cadence is also evident, as in VI, XV and XVII.

Laments of the Professional Mourner

There are numerous rabbinic references indicating that professional mourners were quite common in rabbinic times.[140] First, the laments themselves, as we have already seen, provide internal evidence that they were not the result of spontaneous grief, but were carefuly worked out in advance in accordance with certain fixed forms.

Further evidence for a standardized lament is found in Moed Qatan 25b. At R. Ashi's request, Bar-Kipok, a professional funeral orator, suggests a certain oration for possible use at R. Ashi's funeral. R. Ashi is offended by the use of certain metaphors referring to him, and when R. Ashi dies, Bar-Kipok is not invited to lament for him.

Among the laments by professional orators, certain specific characteristics can be noted. First, the laments sung by the professional women (VII-XIII) are uniformly in Aramaic. By contrast, all the other laments, with one exception, are in Hebrew. This is perhaps because Hebrew was the language of the scholars, while the *lingua franca* of the women was the Aramaic of daily life. The one lament in Aramaic by a man is XIX. However, as the Talmud text indicates, this was uttered not by an Israelite but by an idolator, for whom Hebrew would not have been the natural mode of expression.[141]

There are addition features of the women's laments:

a) We find no record of the women's laments being sung for any specific individual whose name is preserved—as we do in the other laments. They seem to be formulas which could be utilized for any funeral occasion.

b) They are very laconic, and very brief. Two of the recorded laments contain only four words, while the longest (X) is seven words long. They do not express any sharp anguish nor do they reveal a deeply felt grief.

c) At a cursory first glance they appear to be less poetic, in terms of structure, form, technique, than do the other laments. They seem, on the surface, to be rather prosaic and rough-hewn statements of fact. But closer examination uncovers considerable attention to qualities of assonance and alliteration. For example, Lament VIII has the successive guttural *gud garma* in line 1, and the alliterative second line, *v'namti maya l'antikhi*, emphasizing the *tet* in line 1, and juxtaposes—and almost rhymes—*bar rami* with *bar ravrevi* in line 2. Lament X contains a plethora of sibilants in the *shin*, *zadi*, and *taw* of line 1, and the *shin* and *zayin* of line 2. It also contains three *lamedim* in line 1, and two *lamedim* in line 2. In XI, the *zayin* and *peh* sounds are juxtaposed in line 2. Lament XIII effectively expresses resignation in the face of death when it repeats *mutha*. And it contains three *mem* sounds in the first four words.

d) The women's laments, unlike the others, make no allusions to the Bible, referring to it neither in subject matter nor in the phraseology.

e) Of the seven women's laments, three give specific commands (VIII, IX, X); two describe indirectly the assorted vicissitudes of the departed: in XI he has to "borrow his fare" as he manages to scramble aboard the ferry; in XII, the departed are "tested by the goods they sell". In addition, VIII makes an apparent reference to mourning rites.

f) Their images and figures of speech are those of daily life (X, XI, XII, XIII); or they refer to the prevalent mourning customs (VIII, IX, and possibly X).

One further type of rabbinic lament is worthy of note. This type may be labeled the hyperbolic lament. The Talmud, without formally referring to them as laments, records the death of various sages and the effect of their deaths on the natural universe. Thus, Moed Qatan 25b notes that when certain sages died,

—the columns of Caesaria ran with tears, roof gutters ran with blood, stars were visible in the daytime;
—all cedars were uprooted;
—all trees were uprooted;
—fiery stones fell from heaven;
—all images were effaced and were used as stone rollers;
—all statues of humans were torn out of position;
—seventy houses were broken into by thieves at Tiberias;
—hail stones fell from heaven;
—the rocks of the Euphrates kissed each other;
—the rocks of the Tigris kissed each other;
—the palms were laden with thorns.

On the day that Rabbah b. Naḥmani died, "a hurricane lifted an Arab who was riding a camel and transported him from one bank of the River Pappa to the other." [142]

The Lament as an Institution in Rabbinic Times

The significant role played by the lament in rabbinic times is clearly visible in the Talmud. "Whoever weeps for a worthy man is forgiven all his iniquities on account of the honor which he showed him." And "he who does not participate in the eulogy of a good man does not live long." [143] Baba Mezia 86a records a heavenly order to lament for seven days. As one scholar has noted, "weeping over a deceased person has, among the Semites, . . . assumed a character which makes it something different from an immediate manifestation of grief." [144]

So prestigious was the honor of lamenting great scholars that communities jealously guarded these rights. R. Judah ha-Nasi ordered that he not be lamented in the towns, because every town might want to do it and thus begin to quarrel. [145]

Fervent laments were sought after, and it was particularly praiseworthy to arouse grief. For example, if a synagogue was destroyed and grass was now growing on the ruins, the grass could not be cut "so as to arouse grief." [146] In like fashion, children. may be made to rend their clothes for the departed even though children are, strictly speaking, not required to rend. But they may do so "in order to *stir up sadness*." [147] The first three days of mourning contain strict prohibitions against work, for fear that work may cause the mourner to forget to cry. [148] A sage inquires of R. Gamaliel if the "key and ledger of a dead man may be suspended from his coffin in order to *heighten anguish*." [149] According to at least one scholar, the Talmud, though it disapproves of providing the dead with food or personal belongings, nevertheless gave tacit permission to do this in order to make the onlookers grieve more. Therefore, for example, eye-paint is found in some women's graves, as in Beth Sh'arim.[150] And when all is said and done, God Himself weeps and laments, as in Is. 16:6ff., and Jer. 48:29f., where the mourning cries, *y'll, z'ak, h'gh,* are used of God.[151] So important is weeping for the righteous that "whoever sheds tears for a good man, the Holy One blessed be He counts the tears and places them among his treasures."[152]

Although mourning is desirable, it should not be excessive. This is based on Jer. 22:10: "Do not weep for the dead and do not bemoan him," which the Talmud reads as "Do not weep for the dead beyond normal bounds of weeping."[153] Some communities, such as Jerusalem, did not exaggerate the good works of the dead, reciting "only the actual works of the dead before his bier." In Judah, however, "he was eulogized by praise that applied to him and by praise that did not apply to him."[154]

Exaggerated or not, prolonged mourning is presumptuous because man should not be more merciful than the Holy One.[155] And, as we have seen, lamentations are forbidden on a festival.[156]

Everyone is entitled to have a lament recited over him. Ketubot 46b guarantees the right even of a poor man to have no less than two flutes and several wailing women at his funeral.[157]

The institutions of music at the funeral—particularly the flute —and the wailing women are obviously very old. In the "Descent of Ishtar to the Nether World," Tammuz is washed and anointed with oil, and "plays on a flute of lapis."

> When with him the lapis flute . . .
> When with him the wailing men and the
>   wailing women welcome me,
> May the dead rise and smell the incense.[158]

The first cutting of the corn in Egypt and in Canaan were occasions for weeping and wailing, invariably accompanied by a flute. And in a Fifth Dynasty tomb, a man stands piping beside the reapers, evidently playing a dirge lamenting the seasonal disappearance of the fertility gods.[159] The Minoan sarcophagus shows a procession of women led by a flute player, passing a dying bull on the sacrificial table.[160] Evans, following Von Duhn, thinks "that the divinity is charmed down into the tomb . . . with the aid of ritual music played on the double pipes." [161]

That the flute is an extremely old mourning instrument is evident from Sumerian inscriptions. A song lamenting the destruction of Lagash, and another on the ruin of Nippur, are both played on the flute.[162] And Jer. 48:36 clearly associates the sound of a flute or pipe with deep mourning: "My heart moaneth for Moab like pipes for the man of Kir-ḥeres."

It is not clear why the pipe instrument, rather than other instruments, should be associated with mourning. It may be because the flute or pipe possesses a mournful, wailing sound.[163] However, K. Meyer-Baer argues that the Biblical *ḥalil* of Jer. 48:36—like the Greek *aulos*—is a symbol of death and resurrection.[164] Obadiah of Bartenura, a classic commentator on the Mishna, says of Succah 5:1 that the sound of the *ḥalil* used in Temple worship was "more audible" than other instruments.[165]

It is clear that the women who lamented were not simply any women who happened to be present at the funeral, but those with specially trained skills. This is alluded to in Jer. 9:19:

> and teach your daughters wailing,
> and every one her neighbor lamentation.

And in Amos 5:16: ". . . and to lamentation those skilled in wailing."
And in II Sam. 1:24: "Daughters of Israel, weep for Saul." [166]

Several Talmudic sources clearly indicate that the lamenter was a professional who was paid.[167] The institution of *sdeh bokhin* —"the field of weeping"—which was a field outside the city set aside for "weeping before burial," [168] further attests to the carefully planned and formalized features of mourning.[169]

The institution of professional weeping women is also very old and quite universal. Women marched in the New Year parade at Babylon as part of the seasonal wailers.[170] In Egypt, Isis and Nephthys are wailing goddesses over the corpse of Osiris.[171] A woman is the chief celebrant in the Saqqara funeral mastaba.[172] In Syria, Astarte wails over Adonis, and in Asia Minor Cybele laments Attis. On the tomb of Neferhotep is written the following lament of women:

> Woe, woe, hail hail hail hail,
> Lament indefatigably
> Alas what a loss.
> The good shepherd has gone away
> to the land of eternity.[173]

In view of the overwhelming pervasiveness of the wailing women, it is not surprising that the aborigine death practices of Australian tribes also feature them very prominently.[174]

Why the role of women in mourning should be so dominant is discussed by Raphael Patai.[175] He points to the significance of the feminine gender *shekhina*—"the presence of the Divine"— which weeps at the destruction of Jerusalem. Similarly, the Community of Israel (*Knesseth Yisrael,* also feminine) laments over the death and destruction of the Temple.[176] And Jeremiah depicts the wailing and lamenting for the remnants of Israel by using the image of the mother Rachel (Jer. 31:15-17). In Ezekiel 8:14, it is the women who sit weeping for Tammuz.

There is apparently some intrinsic link between women and

death. For example, one student of religious customs echoes a long-standing tradition when he states that since women, through the figure of Eve, are responsible for the "severe judgment" of death upon mankind, they were given the power to overcome the pangs of death by their weeping.[177] This link may account for the fact that women are singled out .in this statement by the Angel of Death:

> Do not stand in front of women when they are returning from the presence of a dead person, because I go leaping in front of them with my sword in my hand and I have permission to harm.[178]

On the other hand, women are endowed with natural gifts for giving comfort. The Rabbis express it thusly:

> R. Shmuel b. Naḥman said: It is the wont of the father to have mercy, "like as a father has compassion upon his children, so has the Lord compassion upon those who fear Him" (Ps. 103:13), and it is the wont of the mother to comfort, "As one whom his mother comforteth, so will I comfort you" (Is. 66:13).[179]

While the Bible makes no specific mention of instrumental music or of dances at funerals, there is evidence for this in certain ancient cultures, as well as in rabbinic literature itself. We know, for example, that the funeral dance was prevalent in Egypt. In "The Tale of Sinuhe" we read: ". . . singers shall open the procession and the dance shall be performed at the door of your grave." [180] Further evidence for the funeral dance is found in the relief from the Saqqara necropolis.[181]

Apparently, funeral dancing in early civilization was motivated by considerations of magic combined with hopes of appeasing the fearsome and hostile dead. For example, the percussion instruments usually shown in Egyptian funeral scenes were probably used for apotropaeic effect.[182]

Why the Bible should be so silent about the funeral dance is
unclear. Perhaps it is because such practices evoked memories
of the pagan fertility cults.[183] However, Gershom Scholem reports
that until quite recently—and occasionally even to this day—
Jewish burials in Jerusalem were marked by "a strange happen-
ing." Before the actual burial, at the graveside, ten men danced
around the grave in a circle, reciting Psalm 91. This dance of
death was repeated seven times.[184] An authoritative medieval text
also writes of funeral dances.[185]

While the Bible is silent, rabbinic literature does refer to the
clapping of the hands and the rhythmic beating of thighs and
other limbs.[186] Furthermore, rabbinic references to certain musical instruments in this connection are quite common. We hear of
the *revi-it,* a kind of drum, and the *halil,* a form of flute or pipe.[187]
Moed Qatan 3:8 and 28b refer to wailing women who, on certain
holy days, may sing the *qinah* but not clap their hands. Moed
Qatan 3:9 mentions certain dirges and hand-clapping as well as
wailing.

It is evident that the laments were accompanied by stamping
on the ground, as in Moed Qatan 27b, which alludes to *tipuah*—
clapping of the hand—and *killus*—tapping with the foot. The
bas-relief on King Ahiram's sarcophagus at Byblos depicts
mourning women, with torn clothes and disheveled hair, who
are slapping their hips.[188]

In addition to the music and dancing, there were several types
of musical laments. In the *'inui* everyone sang together, while in
the *qinah* one began singing alone and then the group responded
after her.[189] Zechariah 12:12-14, "And the land will mourn . . .
the family of the house of David and their wives apart; the family
of the house of Nathan and their wives apart," apparently refers
to a type of antiphonal singing.[190]

CONCLUSIONS

This study of *tum'ah*-defilement legislation in biblical and rabbinic literature began by examining the views of primitive man concerning death. According to many theorists, the overriding element in primitive man's response to death was fear, particularly in relationship to the departed spirits.

Israel's view of death within the context of the Ancient Near East was then established. It was noted that, unlike its neighbors such as Mesopotamia, Canaan, and Egypt, Israel's view of death is shorn of all elements of fear, horror, or ancestor worship. Instead, Israel accepts death as an unavoidable fact of life.

Israel's rigorous defilement legislation—in which a human corpse is the ultimate defilement—seems to raise unusually high barriers against contact with the dead. These barriers, however, are less a manifestation of fear of the dead than an expression of the concept that death removes man from contact with God.

It was pointed out that a non-priest may defile himself through contact with the dead, and by so doing he violates no law. Until his purification, however, he is restricted from participation in the Temple cult. In brief, the dead are divorced from God because they are outside His province and His cult. Contact with the dead desacralizes man and estranges him from God—for the God of life and sanctity represents the ultimate opposite of death

139

and *tum'ah* defilement. God's relationship with man can take place only within the context of life.

The radical desacralization of death and its total removal from the cultic sphere of God finds vigorous expression in biblical and rabbinic legislation concerning cults of the dead. Although neither Bible nor Talmud deny that the dead have certain powers, any human recourse to those powers is stringently prohibited. The laws of *'ob* and *yidde'oni,* as well as those of the other necromancers of Leviticus 19, provide an illustration of such prohibitions. Consistent with Israel's general outlook on death, these prohibitions are not taboos based on dread of the Ancestors, but express the incompatability of the realm of *tum'ah* (death) and God (life).

The details of *tum'ah* are numerous and complex, varying in intensity and category. The most powerful *tum'ah* is death, and it is apparent that whatever is *tamé* and defiles possesses some fundamental connection with death.

The idea of *tamé* as an absence of life and absence of God—desacralization and estrangement—is useful in understanding the frequent use of this term in the Bible. In the dietary regulations of Leviticus 11, for example, unfit foods are referred to as "*tamé.*" But these are not *tamé* in the sense of defilement—since he who eats of the unfit foods is not in need of any purification—but in the pristine sense of "something desacralized"; that is, sacrally unfit for the Israelite's food. Similarly, "*tamé*" in certain other biblical contexts may more felicitously be read as "estranged" or "alien." A number of illustrative passages have been cited in this study.

The biblical/rabbinic legislation concerning the priest and his relationship to death and defilement provides support for this concept of *tum'ah* as estrangement and desacralization. With the exception of members of his immediate family, the priest must be totally removed from any contact with death. Unless it be for the funeral needs of members of his own family (or the unattended *meth mitzvah*—the "obligatory dead"), the priest may not be in the proximity of a corpse, may not be in attendance at a burial, and may not mourn. For the High Priest, the death restrictions are even more severe. This anti-defilement legislation affects the priest exclusively—perhaps because he symbolizes God and sanctity. Because of this, he is not permitted to have contact with death which represents the absence of God and the absence of sanctity.

Despite the barriers existing between defilement and sanctity, there is evidence for some paradoxical kinship between the two. For example, only that can defile which once had the potential of becoming sacred. The most intense *tum'ah* category includes not the creeping things which the Bible scornfully calls an "abomination," but the dead Israelite—who in life had the potential of becoming holy as God is holy. The further one is removed from the cult and potential holiness, the less intense is his power of defiling others. Conversely, those closest to the cult and to God—such as the Israelite—are most defiling, and—in the case of the priest—most susceptible to the restricting consequences of defilement.

In sum, our theoretical examination led to several conclusions:

a) life is a key element in the nature of God, who is *Elo-him hayim*—the Living deity, or the ultimate epitome of life;

b) death, the ultimate absence of life, is a key element in *tum'ah* defilement;

c) death, as the ultimate lifelessness, represents the utmost separation from the God of life—which is desacralization and estrangement;

d) *tum'ah* defilement symbolizes desacralization and estrangement from the Divine.

The second part of our study focuses primarily on the post-biblical mourning legislation as a concrete illustration of these conclusions. The detailed mourning regimen states, in effect, that the mourner—who has come into intimate contact with the realm of death and *tum'ah*—now enters a realm of temporary estrangement from God, from his community, and from himself as a person. His numerous requirements and restrictions as a mourner—which have been traced in detail—are all manifestations of his diminished state as a person. Similarly, the restrictions against fulfilling certain biblical precepts underscore his temporarily desacralized and estranged status: he may not, for example, offer up a sacrifice during the week of mourning; and the laws governing his relationship with other men are manifestations of his estrangement from the community: he may not, for example, extend or receive greetings.

There are clear parallels between the requirements and restrictions of the mourner and the excommunicant. This suggests that the mourner is a symbolic excommunicant, estranged, as is the excommunicant, from the sacred community. Similarly, the legislation concerning *lo'eg larash*—"mocking the dead"—in which certain of God's commandments may not be fulfilled in the presence of the dead, provides further support for the concept of the dead as desacralized.

As was the case in the relationship between defilement and sanctity, so also in the laws of mourning are there numerous indications of a pattern of paradox. Practices governing both mourning and marriage are unusually similar. It is also a remarkable fact that there are no direct biblical laws dealing with mourning requirements for the Israelite. His mourning rites are derived obliquely and indirectly from the priestly legislation in Leviticus, and from specific directives given to the prophet-priest, Ezekiel.

The study closes with a detailed examination of the special characteristics of the rabbinic lament. One of these characteristics, the profane quality of the laments, provides additional support for the idea of the realm of death as estranged and alien from God.

Although the legislation of *tum'ah* in biblical and rabbinic sources has been closely investigated here, the results of this study remain tentative. Much work is still required in the field of defilement as a manifestation of Israel's world view. The subject is as vast as it is complex, and students have unlimited and uncharted territory to reconnoiter.

Over and above the examination of the concept of *tum'ah,* the nature of this study has a wider implication; namely, that the *halakhah*—the biblical and post-biblical legal system—is more than a compendium of legalistic minutiae covering the daily life of the Israelite. The present investigation suggests that this system contains within it certain definite patterns of belief, thought and attitude; in brief, that the *halakhah* is not only law but a world-view as well.

The area of *tum'ah* is perhaps the most complex and recondite in all of biblical and rabbinic law. The fact that a limited inquiry such as this is able to divulge a distinctive *weltanschauung* pre-figures the vast potential of future studies in the field of biblical and rabbinic law.

I conclude this study with the traditional prayer, taken from Isaiah 25:8: "He will destroy death forever, the Lord will wipe away the tear from all faces. . . ."

בלע המות לנצח ומחה ד' דמעה מעל כל פנים...

Notes

1. Throughout this study, the words *tum'ah* and *tamé*—which are sometimes translated as "unclean"—will be translated as, and used synonymously with, "defilement." "Unclean," for reasons that will be made clear, is a somewhat inadequate term.

2. Not all of their works are available in English translation, but see Moses Maimonides, *Guide of the Perplexed,* transl. and ed. by Shlomo Pines (Chicago: 1963); Saadia Gaon, *The Book of Beliefs and Opinions,* transl. and ed. by Samuel Rosenblatt (New Haven, Conn., 1948); Joseph Albo, *Book of Principles* (Philadelphia: 1946); Samson Raphael Hirsch, *Horeb, A Philosophy of Jewish Laws and Observances,* transl. by Dayan I. Grunfeld (London: 1962); Judah Ha-Levi, *Book of Kuzari,* transl. from Arabic by H. Hirschfeld (New York: 1946).

A good summary of the pertinent literature is in Yitzhak Heinemann, *Taamei ha-Mitzvot* (Jerusalem: 1963). To date, this volume is available only in Hebrew.

3. Niddah 9a.

4. Shabbat 31a.

5. Sanhedrin 94b.

6. Sanhedrin 94b, 17a.

7. Erubin 13b.

8. *Midrash Tanḥuma,* ed. Solomon Buber (New York: 1946), Ḥukat, p. 106, par. 7.

9. See Numbers 19.

10. S. Buber, *Midrash Tanḥuma,* p. 118a; Midrash Rabbah (Vilna: 1911), Numbers 19:8, p. 158.

11. Midrash Rabbah to Numbers 9; and *Pesikta Rabbati,* transl. and ed. William G. Braude (New Haven: 1968), I, 14, pp. 289-290.

12. Sanhedrin 68a.

13. Hirsch, *Horeb,* II, par. 118: *"Tum'ah* is that which has sunk outside the human sphere."

14. David Hoffmann, *Vayiqra* (Jerusalem: 1954), I, pp. 215 ff. Jacob Neusner, *The Idea of Purity in Ancient Judaism* (Leiden: 1973), who approaches this subject from a non-theological standpoint, notes a renewed interest in the defilement and purity laws. See his preface, p. xi.

15. In contemporary times R. Joseph B. Soloveitchik is perhaps the most articulate expositor of a philosophy of halakhah. Most of his thought, unfortunately, has yet to be reduced to writing. See Eugene B. Borowitz, *A New Jewish Theology in the Making* (Philadelphia: 1968), pp. 160-173; and Simon Noveck, ed., *Great Jewish Thinkers of the Twentieth Century* (New York: 1963), pp. 281-297, for discussions of R. Soloveitchik's thought. See also, Joseph Epstein, ed., *A Conspectus of the Public Lectures of Rabbi Joseph B. Soloveitchik* (New York: 1974), and Pinchas Peli, ed., *Al Hateshuvah* (Jerusalem: 1975), for transcriptions of some major addresses. The halakhah philosophy of R. Isaac Hutner is available only in Hebrew in the series entitled *Paḥad Yitzḥak* (New York: 1950), and is issued annually since 1950. The late Chief Rabbi of the Holy Land, R. Abraham Kook, also has a series of works on the theme of Jewish law as philosophy, as does the hasidic Lubavitch group, especially R. Menaḥem Mendel of Lubavitch, *Derekh Mitzvosekha* (New York: 1953).

SECTION I

1. James George Frazer, *Fear of the Dead in Primitive Religion,* (London: 1933), I, pp. 11 ff.

2. Ibid., p. 40; and Friedrich von Duhn, "Rot und Tot," *Archiv für Religionwissenschaft* 9 (1906), pp. 124 ff.

3. Adolphe Lods, *La Croyance à la vie future dans l'antique Israélite* (Paris: 1906), p. 220; and *Israel* (New York: 1962), p. 225.

4. William O. E. Oesterley, *Short Survey of the Literature of Rabbinical and Medieval Judaism* (London: 1920), p. 201.

5. Cited in Robert Martin-Achard, *From Death to Life* (Edinburgh: 1960), p. 24.

6. Edwin O. James, *Sacrifice and Sacrament* (London: 1962), p. 161.

7. Helmer Ringgren, *Israelite Religion* (Philadelphia: 1966), p. 239.

8. Louis Finkelstein, *The Pharisees* (Philadelphia: 1938), I, p. 27.

9. Baba Qamma 110b; Ḥullin 133b.

10. Pesaḥim 77a, 79a; Yoma 50b-51a; Maimonides, *Mishneh Torah,* "Laws of Entering the Sanctuary," 4:9, 11. See also, Maimonides, "The Temple," 7:15.

11. Maimonides, "Entering the Sanctuary," 4:12. See, Mishnah Kelim 1:8, 9.

12. Rudolph Otto, *The Idea of the Holy* (London: 1936), p. 127.

13. Mircea Eliade, *Sacred and Profane* (New York: 1961), p. 9.

14. Walther Eichrodt, *Theology of the Old Testament* (Philadelphia: 1967), II, p. 215.

15. Ibid.

16. Lucien Levy-Bruhl, *The Soul of the Primitive* (New York: 1928), p. 239.

17. Lucien Levy-Bruhl, *Primitives and the Supernatural* (New York: 1935), p. 135.

18. Adolphus P. Elkin, *The Australian Aborigines* (London: 1953), p. 301.

19. Frazer, *Fear of the Dead,* III, p. 311.

20. Alfred R. Radcliffe-Brown, *The Andaman Islanders* (Glencoe, Ill.: 1948), p. 299.

21. Sylvia Anthony, *The Child's Discovery of Death* (London: 1940), p. 134.

22. Sigmund Freud, *Thoughts for the Times on War and Death:* 1915 (New York: 1947), pp. 226, 228; see also, his *Totem and Taboo,* transl. John Strachey (New York: 1952). For a good discussion of the ambiguity of death as seen in the thought of Heidegger, see James M. Demske, *Being, Man, and Death: a Key to Heidegger* (Lexington, Ky.: 1970), pp. 194-195.

23. Martin-Achard, *Death to Life,* p. 16.

24. Cited in Jack Goody, *Death, Property, and the Ancestors* (Stanford: 1962), p. 26. See, Robert Hertz, *Death and the Right Hand* (Chicago: 1960), p. 34; 119, n. 36.

25. Mircea Eliade, *Sacred and Profane,* p. 16. On this general theme see M. Haran, "The Taboos of Holiness", *Sefer Segal* (Tel Aviv: 1965), pp. 33-41.

26. See Henri Frankfort, *The Problem of Similarity in Ancient Near East Religions* (Oxford: 1951), p. 28, for a cautionary note about "spurious equations" between cultures.

27. Samuel G. F. Brandon, *The Judgment of the Dead* (New York: 1967), p. 55.

28. Henri Frankfort, *The Birth of Civilization in the Near East* (London: 1951), pp. 20-21.

29. Samuel G. F. Brandon, *Man and His Destiny in the Great Religions* (London: 1962), p. 104. Brandon's point is that the Egyptian view of death is optimistic despite its profound fear of death, since the ritual's main thrust toward physical life after death enables the survivor to feel that he has defeated death completely.

30. Bezalel Porten, *Archives from Elephantine* (Berkeley: 1968), p. 185.

31. Samuel G. F. Brandon, "The Personification of Death in Some Ancient Religions," *BJRL*, 43 (1960-61), p. 320.

32. Brandon, *Judgment of the Dead*, p. 55.

33. E. O. James, *Tree of Life* (Leiden: 1966), pp. 206, 211.

34. E. A. Speiser, *Oriental and Biblical Studies* (Philadelphia: 1967), p. 192.

35. James B. Pritchard, *Ancient Near Eastern Texts* (Princeton: 1950), p. 52, 106.

36. Alexander Heidel, *The Gilgamesh Epic and Old Testament Parallels* (Chicago: 1946), pp. 46; 68-71.

37. Pritchard, *ANET*, p. 90a; p. 54. Samuel Noah Kramer shows that, in the Sumerian belief, the underworld was the "huge cosmic space below the earth corresponding roughly to heaven, the huge cosmic space above the earth"; see his "Sumero-Akkadian Interconnections: Religious Ideas," in *Aspects du Contact Sumero-Akkadien* (Geneva: 1960), p. 280.

38. For an analysis of Canaanite death mythology, see F. F. Hvidberg, *Weeping and Laughter in the Old Testament* (Leiden: 1962), pp. 28-30.

39. Brandon, *Man and His Destiny*, p. 111.

40. Hvidberg, *Weeping and Laughter*, p. 56.

41. William Foxwell Albright, *The Archaeology of Palestine* (London: 1960), p. 93.

42. Yeḥezkel Kaufmann, *The Religion of Israel*, transl. M. Greenberg (Chicago: 1960), p. 304.

43. R. Aharon Ha-Levi, *Sepher Ha-Ḥinukh* (reprinted New York: 1962), I, Commandment 161, p. 149.

44. Maimonides, *Mishneh Torah*, "Laws of Defilement of Foods," 16:8.

45. Moed Qatan 27b.

46. On the relation of sin to death, see below, p. 62.

47. Mishnah Kelim 1:1; Oholot 1.

48. Gerhardt von Rad, *Old Testament Theology* (London: 1963), I, p. 277.

49. See, Genesis 25:8, 35:29, 49:33. For an excellent discussion of death in ancient Israel, see L. Wachter, *Der Tòd im Alten Testament* (Stuttgart: 1964), especially Chapter II.

50. Genesis 25:8, 17; 35:29; 49:33; Numbers 27:13; 31:2; Deuteronomy 32:50. Cf. Jeremiah 8:2; 25:33.

51. Sigmund Mowinckel, *He That Cometh* (New York: 1954), p. 86.

52. Kaufmann, *Religion of Israel* p. 314.

53. See, Edmund Jacob, *Theology of the Old Testament* (New York: 1958), pp. 304 ff., for a fuller discussion of the relevant biblical texts.

54. Cited in A. F. Key, "The Concept of Death in Early Israelite Religion," *JBR*, 32 (1964), pp. 240 ff.

55. Heidel, *The Gilgamesh Epic*, pp. 208-10: See, J. Curtis, "The Mount of Olives in the Judeo-Christian Tradition," *HUCA*, 28 (1957), pp. 146-158, concerning Ishtar's descent; and Pritchard, *ANET*, pp. 52 ff.

56. Kaufmann, *Religion of Israel*, p. 304.

57. Key, "Concept of Death," *JBR*, p. 239.

58. See also, J. A. Sanders, *Dead Sea Psalm Scrolls* (Ithaca: 1967), p. 70: "A maggot cannot praise Thee, nor a graveworm . . . but the living can praise Thee."

59. Shabbat 30a, 151b.

60. For the implications for desacralization of these Talmudic sources, see below pp. 106 ff. the discussion of "mocking the poor," where the inability of the dead to serve God is discussed further.

61. Put another way, death means a relinquishing of all other possibilities. See, John Macquarrie, "True Life in Death," *Journal of Bible and Religion*, 31 (1963): 204-205. Von Rad, *Old Testament Theology*, treats this subject very sensitively (Vol. I, pp. 277 ff.).

62. Ibid., II, p. 350.

63. But see R. David Kimḥi on this chapter, v. 25, in which he states that the woman prepetrated a hoax on Saul, and that she was without any powers in this regard. See also, Maimonides' comment on Mishnah Sanhedrin 7:10, and the comments of Naḥmanides on Deuteronomy 18:9, in Chavel, *Commentary of Naḥmanides*, II, p. 427.

64. Leviticus 19:27, 31; 20:6, 27; 21:5; Dt. 14:1; 12:11; 26:14.

65. Baba Mezia 107d.

66. Saul Lieberman, "Afterlife in Early Rabbinic Literature," in *Harry A. Wolfson Jubilee Volume II* (New York: 1965), p. 511, suggests that she asked for these cosmetics because she wanted to be ready for resurrection. He cites J. Kilaim, IX. 4, 32b; Ketubot 111b; Sanhedrin 90b; Semahot IX. For other instances of burial on public roads and preparing for the Messiah, see, Genesis Rabbah 80:10 and J. Kilaim IX. 4, 32b.

67. Shabbat 152a-b.

68. Sotah 34b; but cf. Ber. 18b-19a.

69. Sanhedrin VII:7.

70. See also, Sifra, *ad loc.*

71. Sanhedrin, 65a-b.

72. On Leviticus 26:4, p. 371.

73. Eichrodt, in *Theology,* p. 215, refers to the Arabic cognate for *'ob,* which is *'w-b,* "to return."

74. See their respective comments on Mishnah Sanhedrin 7:7.

75. Shabbat 152b.

76. G. van der Leeuw, *Religion in Essence and Manifestation* (New York: 1938), pp. 292-293.

77. Heidel, *Gilgamesh Epic,* pp. 199-200.

78. Ibid., pp. 201 ff.

79. Sanhedrin, 65b.

80. Tosefta Sanhedrin, ch. 10, and J. Sanhedrin, 7:10.

81. Maimonides, *Mishneh Torah,* "Laws of Idolatry," 11:13; "Laws of Sanhedrin," 11:4.

82. The Rabbis require a man to stand on his feet while the corpse passes by in a funeral cortege, but they explain that this is not because we stand before the dead, "but before those who attend to his burial needs." See J. Kiddushin 3, 65c; Kiddushin 33a.

83. See T. ·C. Mitchell, "The Old Testament Usage of *Neshama,*" VT 11 (1961), pp. 177-178, who points out that *neshama* describes the "breath of God," which, when given to man, makes him unique. See also, Daniel Lys "The Israelite Soul According to the LXX," VT 16 (1966), pp. 181 ff., which discusses how the Greek translators read the word *nefesh;* and see below, note 92.

84. Martin-Achard, *Death to Life,* p. 5.

85. Baba Qama 65a.

86. David S. Russell, *The Method and Message of Jewish Apocalyptic* (London: 1964), p. 353. He goes on to suggest that the *rephaim* of

Genesis may refer to "weak ones," those bereft of life. Note also similar usages in the Talmud, as in Yebamoth 55b, and Shabuot, 18a.

87. Sanhedrin 74a; Ketubot 19a. The three for which even life must be sacrificed rather than that they be violated, are: idolatry, murder, and adultery/incest.

88. Harris Birkeland, "The Belief in the Resurrection of the Dead in the O.T.," *Studia Theologica*, 3, (1951): p. 69.

89. Thorlief Boman, *Hebrew Thought Compared with Greek* (Philadelphia: 1960), p. 27; cited in Hwa Yol Jung, "The Logic of the Personal: John Macmurray and the Ancient Hebrew View of Life," *The Personalist* 47 (1966), p. 41. In general, Hwa's article is an excellent presentation of the actional aspects of biblical thought.

90. See A. R. Johnson, *The Vitality of the Individual in the Thought of Ancient Israel* (Cardiff: 1949), pp. 9-26; 26-39, for discussion of *nefesh*.

91. Harry M. Orlinsky, *Notes on the New Translation of the Torah* (Philadelphia: 1969), p. 60.

92. It might simply mean, "up to the nostrils," or "until the breathing." Note also that *nefesh* means desire," as in Exodus 15:9: "my desire (*nafshi*) is fulfilled." And see Deuteronomy 12:15: "the desire (*'abath*) of your *nefesh*," repeated several times in this section and elsewhere. Note also that *hayah*, "life" or "livingness," is often used together with *nefesh*, as in Genesis 1:20 ff.; 19:20. See also, IK. 20:32; Jeremiah 38:20; Psalms 119 and 175, among other references. See above, note 83.

93. L. Silberman, in Liston O. Mills, ed. *Perspectives on Death* (Nashville, 1969), p. 17.

94. *Ibid.,* p. 19.

95. Midrash Rabbah Exodus 3:6 (Berlin, Horeb edition), p. 250. While the purpose of this Midrash is to indicate that the essence of the deity in unknowable, it simultaneously illustrates the rabbinic emphasis on His actions.

96. Mekhilta of R. Yishmael (Vienna: 1870), p. 219.

97. Shabbat 152b. See, *The Fathers According to Rabbi Nathan,* transl. Judah Goldin (New Haven: 1955), chap. 26, p. 111. For the implications of burial "under the Throne of Glory," or "under the altar," see Saul Lieberman, *Hellenism in Jewish Palestine* (New York: 1950), pp. 161 ff.

98. Shabbat 88b; Midrash Rabbah Genesis 88:10; 28:8.

99. Rosh Hashanah 4:5. See, Ephraim Urbach, *The Sages* (Hebrew) (Jerusalem: 1969), pp. 54 ff, to whom I am indebted for an excellent review of this theme. An English translation appeared in 1974.

100. Shabbat 88b.

101. Ibid., 87a.

102. See also, Leviticus 11:44, 18:25, 20:25 in which the ultimate reason for avoiding *tum'ah* is "because I the Lord am holy."

103. See also, Leviticus 35:34.

104. Abodah Zarah 20b; see also, Abodah Zarah 39a.

105. Leviticus 19:11, 14, 16; Baba Qama 2b; See also, Rashi's comment to Pesachim 14b; Mishnah Kelim 1:4, as well as Rashi's comment to Numbers 19:22.

106. Throughout this study, we will use the term "ultimate category" instead of the literal "father of fathers."

107. Mishnah Kelim 1:2.

108. Ibid., 1:1.

109. Leviticus 15; Deuteronomy 23:11; Mishnah Kelim 1:5; Mishnah Zabim 5:11. The use of "leper" is a loose translation for the Hebrew *mezora,* which bears only a tangential connection with leprosy as we know it today.

110. Mishnah Kelim 2:1.

111. This is the term we will be using instead of the more literal "father of defilement". An *'ab* is that grade of *tum'ah* which is intensive enough to convey its defilement to man or vessels by touch.

112. Mishnah Kelim 1:1.

113. *Ohel* literally means "tent." Tent defilement can be conveyed by a corpse to men or utensils which are under the same tent or roof, even if there is a partition between the body and the clean person.

114. Kelim 1:4; Oholot 2:1; Numbers 19:14. Although a leper also conveys defilement by *ohel,* this is only where there is no partition. For further differences between a leper's and a corpse's *ohel,* see J. Lipshitz ("Tifereth Israel"), *Introduction to Order Toharot* in every standard Mishnah. Soncino Mishnah Kelim, p. 9, note 6 and 7, presents a convenient summary in English.

115. Mishnah Oholot 1, 1:4; Numbers 19:11, 22.

116. Kelim 2:1 and see *ibid.,* 17:13.

117. Mishnah Makhshirin 6:4, and commentary of Tifereth Israel *ad. loc.* For a convenient English translation of Elijah of Vilna's classic sum-

mation of the defilement legislation, see Herbert Danby, *The Mishnah* (London: 1933), pp. 800-804.

118. See, Maimonides, *Mishneh Torah*, "Miqvaoth" ("Ritual Immersion"), 1 ff.

119. So powerfully *tamé* is death that, according to one rabbinic opinion, mere distress because of a kinsman's death can make one *tamé*, apparently even without contact with the corpse. See, J. Pesaḥim 8, 8:7.

120. Remarkable support for the concept of *tamé* as antilife is found in Rashi's comment on Leviticus 11:1, "these are the beasts (*ḥayah*) which you may eat. . . ." Rashi cites Midrash Tanḥuma in his exegesis of the word *ḥayah*, which, he says, is from the root *ḥayim*, "life." The fact that the text uses this term, and not the more obvious *"behemah,"* for beast, is because "Israel cleaves to the Lord and is worthy of being in a state of *ḥayim* (life), *therefore He separated them from* tum'ah" (italics added).

121. Oholot 2:1; and see, 2:5 with Obadiah of Bartenura's gloss; Bekhorot 45a; Sifra *Torat Kohanim, Shmini,* p. 149, par. 2; *Yalqut Shimoni,* Numbers 19, par. 762, p. 517, col. b.

122. Yoma 81b; Sanhedrin 4a; BQ 101b.

123. Chavel, ed. *Commentary of Naḥmanides on the Torah* II, Leviticus, p. 85, note 2. See also Judah Ha-Levi's *Book of Kuzari*, transl. from the Arabic by H. Hirschfeld (New York: 1936), part II, sec. 60, for an English language discussion on this theme. Jacob Neusner, *The Idea of Purity in Ancient Judaism* (Leiden: 1973), pp. 41, ff., reviews some early allegorical interpretations of seminal defilement.

124. *Commentary of Rikanati* (Gross Publ.: Brooklyn, N.Y., offprint of original Lublin edition, 1595) p. 24b.

125. J. Berakhot 3:4.

126. Leviticus 15; 19-33; Berakhot 26a, 31b; Shabbat 32a; and Tractate Niddah. For the views of a classical cabbalist concerning the defilement of menstrual blood, see Naḥmanides, "Torat Ha-adam," in Chavel, *Kitvei Ramban* II, pp. 104-105.

127. See also Genesis 9:4, where *nefesh* is equated with blood. A small amount of blood is equivalent to a body and may defile (Sanhedrin 4a). The almost universal use of the color red in connection with death and burial in primitive cultures has been explained by some scholars as being a symbolic attempt to restore life to the dead by the use of blood or its surrogate, red. Thus, S. G. F. Brandon, in *Man and his Destiny* p. 11, after noting that some Upper Paleolithic skulls show traces of red ochre,

and that numerous Paleolithic skeletons have evidence of the red color, states that the purpose of the color red was magical, since it is the color of blood which was thus "symbolically restored to it." Edwin O. James, *Comparative Religion* (New York: 1961), p. 92, writes of "smearing the corpse with blood or its surrogate red ochre . . . prompted by . . . a desire to impart life to the body.

Although they are not within the purview of this study, there are numerous attestations to the use of red in death and mourning among primitives. See Bronislav Malinowski, *The Family Among the Australian Aborigines* (New York: 1969), p. 271, about the use of red in the dress of mourners; Gaster, in *Thespis: Ritual, Myth, and Drama in the Ancient Near East* (New York: 1961), p. 210, who cites the Ugaritic Baal poem: "puissant Baal . . . in thy hand red ochre." Gaster makes numerous references to varied usages of red. See also Rachel Levy, *Religious Conceptions of the Stone Age*, p. 69, and p. 235, concerning the Minoan sarcophagus showing a priestess pouring blood into a jar; S. Piggot, *The Dawn of Civilization* (New York: 1961), p. 34, discusses Bavarian skills of the fourth millennium dyed with red ochre, and a red parapet that surrounds the corpse (p. 43).

Archeological attestations for the use of red in graves are also to be found in Paul W. Lapp, "The Cemetery at Bab edh-Dhra' Jordan," in *Archeological Discoveries in the Holy Land* (New York: 1967) which discusses red-burnished jugs in twenty-fourth-century tombs on p. 38, and Beth Shearim catacomb inscriptions in red, p. 181; *JNES* 3 (1944), p. 202, about red linen used for the body; *IEJ* 1 (1950-51), p. 94, about red lamps in a Carthage necropolis; *IEJ* 5 (1955); p. 215; 221-222: a bilingual red inscription in the Beth Shearim acrosolium; *IEJ* 9 (1959), p. 207: further inscriptions in red; *Southwest Journal of Anthropology*, 24 (1968), p. 145: red ochre is common in Near East in Upper Paleolithic; *IEJ* 13 (1963), p. 302: Paleolithic and Chalcolithic burial caves with red-slabbed tombstones.

The connection of the color red with blood and life is stressed by Rachel Levy, *Stone Age*, p. 64: "Blood was the physical counterpart of the mystical life-union. It was probably represented in the red ochre painted over the sacred bone. . . ." Bruno Bettelheim, *Symbolic Wounds* (Glencoe, Ill.: 1954), p. 169, writes that among the aborigines, "red ochre is not simply symbolic . . . in its extensive ceremonial use red ochre must be considered to be menstrual blood or else very closely related to it." See also Stith Thompson, *Motif-Index of Folk-Literature* (Bloomington:

1933), II, pp. 98-99 #D1003, that blood can cure, restore sight, resuscitate, and is a life token. Von Duhn, "Rot und Tot," pp. 124ff., evidently had an important influence on later research on the subject of red and death.

128. "There are four who are similar to a dead man: a pauper, a leper, a blind man, and he who has no children." Nedarim 64b; Midrash Rabbah Genesis 1:9. Also Judah Ha-Levi, *Kuzari,* II:60, "A dead body represents the highest degree of malignancy, and a leprous limb is as if dead."

129. J. Moed Qatan 3:5.

130. Negaim 1:1 ff.

131. Described above, p. 49, in footnote 113.

132. The leper, with his festering boils and blisters, evidently gives off bodily secretions as well: Negaim 7:1, 9:1. These secretions are not, of course, life-giving. For the Midrashic interpretation of the moral significance of the leper's purification rites, see, Midrash Rabbah Numbers 19:3, (Vilna ed.), p. 156, col. b.

133. A symbolic reading of the death purification rites is found in Naḥmanides, "Torat Ha'adam," in Chavel *Kitve Ramban II.*

134. Mourner and excommunicant have a similar relationship, with important implications. See below, pp. 104-106.

135. Moed Qatan 14-16a.

136. See, Berakhot 22a.

137. These various restrictions will be discussed in detail in the chapter on mourning legislation, pp. 84-86.

138. Moed Qatan 15b.

139. Negaim 3:1.

140. Ibid., 12.1; 11:1; 7:1; see also Gittin 82a.

141. Negaim 12:1. It is also significant that only leprosy proclaimed as such by the *kohen* defiles, based on Leviticus 13:2-3, especially "and . . . the priest shall see him and pronounce him unclean," and Sifra *ad loc:* "Defilement and purification of leprosy is only by proclamation of the priest." But see *Sheiltot of R. Aḥai Gaon* (Jerusalem: Mossad Harav Kook, 1961) on Sidrah Mezora, p. 111, for an apparently different view. Similarly supra-hygienic is Leviticus 13:12-13, in which a man who breaks out with leprous signs over the entire body is clean, whereas if he has a single "bright spot" upon him, he is defiled. See on this passage, Midrash Rabbah Numbers 9:1, which declares: "None other than the Holy One could have decreed this." See also below, pp. 66-67.

142. Moed Qatan 15a.

143. The meaning of "or a man through whom he can be rendered unclean" is this: "or a dead man through whom, etc." See comment of Rashi *ad loc.*

144. Numbers 19:8, 10, 22; Mishnah Parah 4:4.

145. Midrash Rabbah Numbers 19:4; Pesikta Rabbati 14:14, transl. Williams G. Braude (New Haven: 1968), I, p. 292.

146. Midrash Tadshe, 17, cited in M. D. Gross, *Ozar Ha-'aggadah,* (Jerusalem: 1954), II, p. 904. See also, Midrash Rabbah Numbers 19:8 (Vilna ed.), p. 158.

147. For an illuminating discussion as to how the specific details of the Red Heifer are connected with the Golden Calf, see Solomon Buber, ed., *Midrash Aggadah* (Lvov: 1890; reprinted Jerusalem: 1961), pp. 244-247; and *Midrash R. Moshe Ha-darshan,* cited in Rashi's commentary on Numbers 19.

148. Leviticus 16:26; Yoma 672-68a.

149. Leviticus 16:21-22.

150. Rab and Samuel dispute this point in Yoma 67a-b: "Are those limbs [of the dashed he-goat] permitted for general use?"

151. Yoma 66a.

152. Buber, ed., *Midrash Tanhuma,* p. 183.

153. Hoffmann, *Vayiqra,* pp. 220, 317.

154. See, S. Buber, ed., *Midrash Tanhuma, Vayeshev,* 4, where death was established as a fact of life in the world even prior to creation. See also, *Tanhuma, Vaeth-hanan,* 6: "For all creatures, death has been prepared from the beginning"; Shabbat 55b: "There is death without sin"; and Nahmanides on Genesis 2:17: "'Man was destined for death from the beginning of creation."

The general subject of sin and death is beyond the scope of this study. But see *Yalqut Shimoni* I, 764, concerning Adam's sin and death. On the same theme see, Haim Schwarzbaum, "Jewish, Christian, Moslem, and Falasha Legends of the death of Aaron, the High Priest," *Fabula* 5-6 (1962), p. 192, and Wolf Leslau, *Falasha Anthology* (New York: 1969), p. 28; N. K. Gottwald, *Studies in the Book of Lamentations* (London: 1954), p. 50f.; David Daube, "Concessions to Sinfulness in Jewish Law," *JJS,* X (1959), pp. 1-13. On the question of death without sin, see also Karl Rahner, "Theology of Death," in *Modern Catholic Thinkers,* ed. A. R. Caponigri (London: 1960), p. 152. See also, A. Buchler, *Studies in Sin and Atonement in the Rabbinic Literature of the First Century* (reprinted New York: 1967).

155. See, *Midrash on Psalms* 51:2: "Whoever commits a sin, it is as if he defiled himself with a corpse." Helmer Ringgren, *Faith of Qumran* (Philadelphia: 1963), pp. 123 ff.; points out that sin in Qumran is like defilement.

156. Yoma 67b.

157. Cited in *Kitvei Rabbenu Bahya,* ed., Charles P. Chavel, (Jerusalem: 1969), p. 41. But the editor, in footnote 11, writes: "I have not found this particular Midrash on the Psalms 82 passage," and goes on to cite *Pirke d'R. Eliezer ha-Gadol* 22, where there is an allusion to angels "who fell from the place of their sanctity from heaven."

158. Sifra, *Aharei,* 2:6, Leviticus (Jerusalem: 1969), II, p. 45.

159. Midrash Rabbah (Berlin: 1927), p. 365.

160. Ibid., p. 257.

161. See Chavel, ed., *Nahmanides,* "Torat Ha-adam," who says that *'azazel* is a sacrifice to the "Force of Esau." Esau represents estrangement from the essence of Israel.

162. Abodah Zarah 5:1, Shabbat 9:1; J. Pesahim. 3:36, 3; "They made the defilement of idolatry similar to the defilement of bodily emissions and the leper"; Toharot 5:8; Shabbat 83b; J. Shabbat 9:11; J. Abodah Zarah 3:43, 2:4; J. Pesahim 36:2.

See also Maimonides, *Mishneh Torah,* "Laws of Principal Categories of Defilement," 6:5: "All things used for the service of idolatry convey defilement to man and vessels through touch. . . ." See also Nahmanides' reading of Genesis 35:4, "and Jacob hid them [the foreign gods] under the terebinth which was by Shechem." Nahmanides comments, "Idolatry and those things used for it do not require burial, but they have to be taken apart and thrown to the winds or into the seas." He cites Abodah Zarah 43b as the source, and adds: "The idolator must destroy the idol even against his will." See Abodah Zarah 52b. Pesikta Zutrati, Genesis 35b, contains essentially the same thought as Nahmanides.

163. See also, Ezekiel 20:18, 26:18, 37:23; Zechariah 13:2.

164. See, Joel 4:17, where *zarim,* "strangers (clearly heathens) will no longer pass through" Jerusalem in which God dwells on His holy mountain; and Zechariah 14:21: "And the Canaanite will no longer be in the house of God."

165. Toharot 5:8; Shabbat 127b; J. Abodah Zarah 5:15; See Abodah Zarah 75b.

166. Toharot 4:5; Oholot 18:7; Maimonides, *Mishneh Torah,* "Laws of Death Defilement," 2:15.

167. Ibid.

168. On the subject of the defilement of foreign soil, see the seminal study of A. Buchler, "The Levitical Impurity of the Gentiles," JQR n.s. XVII, p. 1-81. Buchler's major theses, among which is the idea that defilement was decreed upon Gentiles because of Jewish nationalistic considerations, are effectively refuted by Gedalyahu Allon, *Mehqarim Betoldot Yisrael* I (Tel Aviv: 1970), pp. 121 ff. Allon concludes, (pp. 144 ff.) citing Joshua 22:19, and Amos 4:17, that the "defilement of foreign soil was not originally because of doubts concerning their dead, but because of a defilement of heathens which includes even their lands."

169. Maimonides, *Mishneh Torah,* "Death Defilement," 2:13.

170. Mary Douglas, *Purity and Danger* (New York: 1966), pp. 77 ff.

171. Ibid., pp. 49, 51. See also, Mary Douglas, "Deciphering a Meal," *Daedalus,* Winter, 1972, pp. 61-82, in which she posits the same theory. For a good review of early allegorical interpretations of the biblical dietary laws, see S. Stein, "The Dietary Laws in Rabbinic and Patristic Literature," in K. Aland and F. Cross, eds., *Studia Patristica* II (Berlin: 1957), pp. 141-154.

172. Pedersen, *Israel,* III, p. 19. See also, Pedersen I-II, p. 491: "Clean is what belongs to the psychic totality, unclean that which counteracts it."

173. Douglas, *Purity,* p. 53; "Deciphering a Meal," p. 74.

174. Ibid., pp. 55 ff; "Decpihering," p. 74.

175. Maimonides, *Mishneh Torah* "Categories of Defilement," 1:1-3; See, Leviticus 11:39.

176. Sanhedrin 17b; Erubin 13b; and see, *Sepher Ha-ḥinukh,* I, Commandment 159, p. 293.

177. Cited above, in Introduction, p. 4. Herold S. Stern, "The Ethics of the Clean and the Unclean," *Judaism* V, 1957, pp. 319-327, presents a rather unified view of the dietary laws without creating artificial categories.

178. *Interpreter's Bible* (Nashville: 1953), II, Leviticus, pp. 94 ff.

179. One may, however, contract defilement by *eating* carrion of a clean fowl, even though contact with it after its death does not defile. (Toharot 1:1) Contact with carrion of *unclean* or forbidden beasts or fowl, as in Leviticus 11:24 ff, does defile and would need purification.

180. Makkot 3:1, see, Zeb. 34a-b, and Maimonides, *The Book of Commandments,* trans. Charles B. Chavel (London: 1957), II, "Negative Commandments," #172 ff., pp. 167 ff.

181. The Rabbis insist that one should refrain from eating pig, not

because he does not like it, but because it is divinely prohibited. See, Sifra on Leviticus 20:26.

182. See, *lakhem* in Lev. 11: 6, 7, 8, 10, 11, 12, 20, 23, 26, 27, 28, 29, 31.

183. See also, Leviticus 15:31; Leviticus 20:3; Psalms 79:1; 2 Chronicles 36:14.

184. See also, Isaiah 57:15; Habakkuk 3:3; Hosea 11:9; Psalms 22: 43; Psalms 99:3, among many other references. See Eliezer Berkovits, *Man and God* (Detroit: 1969) pp. 173 ff., for a discussion of the idea of *qadosh* in the Bible.

185. Taanit 11a. But see, Nedarim 10a, where R. Elazar ha-Kappar reads Numbers 6:11, "the priest shall make an atonement for him [the Nazarite] because he hath sinned against a soul. . . ." in a totally different way: the Nazarite is called a sinner because he deliberately afflicts himself concerning one thing, wine; how much more so is he a sinner who denies himself the enjoyment of many things. "Hence, one who fasts [needlessly] is called a sinner."

The contradictory comments are too similar in form to be a coincidence. Baruch HaLevy Epstein, in his *Torah Temimmah* (New York: 1928) "Numbers", p. 66, n. 47, attempts to reconcile the two, based on Taanit 11b: "one passage refers to him who is able to bear affliction, and othe other to him who is not able."

See Nazir 19a, on Numbers 6:11: "against what soul did he sin? It can only be because he denied himself wine. If this man who denied himself wine only is termed a sinner, how much more so is this true of one who is ascetic in all things."

186. Braude, transl., *Pesiqta Rabbati,* p. 265, based on the lengthier discussion in Pesaḥim 3a-b. See also, Rashi's comment on Genesis 7:2.

187. Ibid., p. 267.

188. Emor 26:1.

189. See also, S. Buber, *Midrash Tanḥuma,* Numbers, Ḥukat, par. 6, p. 105.

190. *The Midrash on Psalms,* transl. William G. Braude, (New Haven: 1959), 1:3.

191. See Deuteronomy 18:5; Numbers 16:5.

192. Sifra, ed. by Yisrael Meir Ha-Cohen (reprinted Jerusalem: 1969-70), *Tazria'* 1:9, p. 181.

193. Vol. I, p. 295.

194. Sifra; see also, *Sh'iltot of R. Aḥai Gaon* (Vilna, reprinted in Jerusalem: 1961) Leviticus, p. 225.

195. Bekhorot 45b.

196. See on this passage, Sifra to Emor 1:13. See, Maimonides, *Guide of the Perplexed,* III:47, p. 596.

197. Leviticus 21:12; Zeb. 28; see also, Maimonides, *Mishneh Torah* "Laws on Entering the Sanctuary," 2:6, and comments on Ibn Daud and Keseph Mishnah *ad loc.;* see, Chavel, ed., *The Commandments,* II, p. 160; see also Sem. 4:6: defilement for the priest's own family "is not a matter of choice—it is mandatory."

198. Berakhot 32b.

199. For a discussion on barring the unworthy from entering sacred sites in Babylon and Egypt, see Shalom Spiegel, "A Prophetic Attestation of the Decalogue," *HTR* 27 (1934), pp. 120 ff.

200. See Mishnah Moed Qatan 1:2; the Talmud's commentary on this Mishnah indicates that this was a very ancient practice, even antedating Ezekiel. See Ezekiel 39:15, ". . . when anyone seeth a man's bones, then shall he set up a sign by it. . . ."; MQ 5b discusses various requirements for the special grave signs. See also J. Rothschild, "The Tombs of Sanhedria," *PEQ* 84, (1952), p. 25.

201. See, Midrash Rabbah Genesis 96-100; *Midrash Tanḥuma,* Buber, ed., 105-17; *Myth and Legend of Ancient Israel,* ed., A. S. Rappaport (New York: 1966), II, p. 162.

202. Haim Schwartzbaum, "Legends of the Death of Aaron, the High Priest," in *Fabula: Zeitschrift für Erzahlforschung,* 5-6 (1962), pp. 190-191.

203. Ibid., p. 206; see, Jellinek, *Bet Hamidrash,* I, pp. 91-95; and *Yalqut Shimoni,* I, 34.

204. Sanhedrin 2:1: The reason for this prohibition is that he not be tempted to touch it and thereby defile himself.

205. See, Maimonides, *Commandments,* II, p. 155, who explicitly states that priests are forbidden "to enter the Sanctuary with disheveled hair, *in the fashion of mourners. . . .*" (italics added). It is apparent from a number of sources, such as Sanhedrin 22b, and Maimonides, "Entrance Into the Sanctuary" I: 8-17, that an underlying motif for the prohibition against the priest's overgrown hair in the Temple is that it represents a form of personal degradation (*nivul*) unbecoming a priest or the Temple. The mourner's requirement to allow his hair to grow long is perhaps due to this same consideration: the mourner is required to demonstrate *nivul*.

Ultimately, then, the long hair is unbecoming for the Temple because it is an act of mourning. See below pp. 94 ff., for a full discussion of mourning rites as depersonalization, of which *nivul* is one manifestation.

206. Sifra on Leviticus 10:6, 13:5, and 21:10.

207. Bekhorot 45b.

208. For a history of the term *met mitzvah,* see D. Zlotnick, ed., *The Tractate Mourning* (New Haven: 1966), p. 21.

209. Nazir 43b.

210. Nazir, 47-48; Megillah 3b; Sifra *Leviticus, Emor* 11:4, p. 100; See, also, Maimonides, *Mishneh Torah* "Laws of the Mourner," 3:8.

211. Sifra, on Leviticus p. 96.

212. Exodus Rabbah 18:8; 15:5. See Berakhot 19b-20a on *kabod habriot* and the *met mitzvah.*

213. Megillah 3b; Shabbat 71b, 94b; Berakhot 19b; Erubin 41b; Menahot 37b.

Closely related to the concept of *kabod habriot* is the idea of *kabod hamet*—"dignity of the dead"—which must be maintained at all costs. Levity in the burial grounds is forbidden because of *kabod hamet* (Megillah 29a). The faces of the poor are to be covered with a sheet in order not to shame those whose faces may be black with hunger (Moed Qatan 27a). He who transfers the remains of the dead from place to place must treat them with proper respect (Berakhot 18a; Semahot 13). If the deceased has left a will that asks for cremation, and that the ashes be used for fertilizer, the will is invalid (J. Ketubot 11, 1:34b; Sanhedrin 46b; Shebi'it 3:1). Short cuts may not be taken through burial grounds (Semahot 14); no bodily needs may be met (J. Berakhot 2:3); no shepherding of beasts or digging of irrigation canals are permitted (Megillah 29a).

214. Megillah 26b.

215. Babba Qama 71a; Sotah 45b; Sanhedrin 47b.

216. See, Isaiah 59:2: "Your sins have made a separation between you and your Lord."

217. Citations from the *Zohar* are taken from Samuel of Sokhotsov, *Shem Mishmuel, Exegesis on the Pentateuch* (Heb.), (Jerusalem: 1952 edition), III, Leviticus, *Emor* pp. 307 ff.

218. Mishnah Abot 1:12.

219. It is because of this, suggests the *Zohar,* that the priest may not marry a divorcee, because a divorcee represents separation, apartness, a tearing asunder of two cleaving forces: "and they shall be one flesh."

220. See, Chavel, ed., *Naḥmanides,* II, p. 116. Naḥmanides remarks that the precept *qedoshim tiheyu* ("ye shall be holy") in Leviticus 19:1, means *not* to become *tamé,* even though "we are not prohibited from it."

221. The *ḥaber* must also avoid death defilement, but not as absolutely as a priests. The *ḥaber*—literally, "associate"—is a member of a group which obligates itself to special scrupulousness in religious practice, with emphasis on tithing and purification. The *ḥaber* is therefore very similar, in this regard, to a priest. For further laws of the *ḥaber,* see Mishnah Demai II:3.

222. Maimonides, *Commandments,* I, commandment 109, p. 118; see also, Maimonides, *Guide,* III: 47, p. 595.

223. See, Berakhot 14b; Semaḥot 13:4.

224. Hoffmann, *Vayiqra,* p. 221.

225. This theory is somewhat inconsistent, since a *sherez*—a "crawling thing"—which is hardly similar to man in form, is involved in *tum'ah.*

226. Yebamot 61a; see above, p. ....., about the laws of *'ohel.*

227. Baba Meẓia 114b; Maimonides, *Mishneh Torah,* "Death Defilement" 1:12-15. See also, Soncino ed. of Yebamot, p. 405, n. 2.

228. Theodorus Vriezen takes interesting issue with the normative scholarly reading of *qdsh* as "separate," finding it too narrow and negative to be used of God. He states that the etymology is either the idea of "brilliance" or "separation." For him, the most plausible meaning is "to be brilliant, so that man cannot behold it," after the Babylonian. See Th. Vriezen, *An Outline of Old Testament Theology* (Oxford: 1958), p. 149, n. 2; p. 150.

229. Mishnah Yadaim 3:2-4; 4:5. This type of *tum'ah* is a rabbinic decree designed to discourage the handling of certain sacred objects. If an individual knows that he will become *tamé,* he will refrain from such handling.

230. This is reminiscent of Eliade's insistence that death symbolizes the passing into a stage of sacredness rather than profaneness. See, Eliade, *Sacred and Profane,* p. 9. If death is sacred as well as defiling, it is not surpising, given our thesis that only the most sacred can become the most defiling, that death is the ultimate defilement.

231. Most classical exegetes follow the rabbinic reading of *lo 'eḥad* as referring to the One. Note that Targum Pseudo-Jonathan, *ad loc.,* also translates it in this way.

232. Niddah 9a.

233. Midrash Rabbah on Numbers 9:1.

234. Yalqut Shimoni, Ḥukat, p. 515, citing Sifri Zuta.

235. Midrash Rabbah Numbers 19:5, p. 157.

236. See also, Yoma 67b; S. Buber, ed., *Midrash Tanḥuma* Numbers, Ḥukat, 4 p. 103, also lists a similar series of paradoxes dealing specifically with *tum'ah;* see also Yalqut Shimoni on this subject.

237. Kelim, I, esp. Mishnah 6-9. See *Zohar* on Leviticus 41 (Shmini), which discusses the relationship between purity and defilement. See also, commentary of R. Shmuel Edles ("Maharsha") on Kelim I.

238. The rabbinic authority and mystic, R. Loewe of Prague (1520-1609), in his discussion of the concept of "opposites," reads Job 14:4 precisely in this way. See A. Kariv, ed., *Kitve Maharal Mi-Prague* ("The Writings of Maharal of Prague"), (Jerusalem: 1960), I, pp. 32-33; see above, pp. 66-67 for a fuller treatment of this Job passage.

239. Ezekiel 24:17; MQ 15b, 21a.

240. According to Sanhedrin 47b, the natural soil of a grave is permitted; but see, Megillah 29a, where even the natural soil of burial ground is prohibited from one's personal use "out of respect for the dead."

241. See also, Baba Mezia 55b; Kiddushin 56b; Keritot 1:1; 6a, 22a, 26b; Nazir 4:3; Yoma 20a; Zebaḥim 85b ff.

242. Me'ilah 2:2, 3; See, Kiddushin 57a and Sanhedrin 47b, concerning the broken-necked heifer of Deuteronomy 21:1-9, which becomes forbidden the moment it is designated.

243. Midrash Rabbah Leviticus 20, p. 58.

244. Sanhedrin 47b, and see, Berakhot 18b; Shabbat 13b; see also, Jellinek, *Bet Ha-Midrash*, I, p. 151.

245. Sanhedrin 46b; see L. Y. Rahmani, "Jewish Rock-cut Tombs in Jerusalem," *'Atiqot* 3, (1961), pp. 117-118, n. 2, for discussion of burial and decay as expiation; and R. Isaac Ha-Levi Herzog, "On the Law of Burying as Apostate," in *No'am* (Jerusalem: 1959), II, pp. 1-13, on the theme of burial as expiation.

246. Mircea Eliade's views about the *sanctity of death* are pertinent here. In his *Yoga, Immortality and Freedom* (New York: 1958), p. 364, he writes that Yoga participates and initiates man into death "in order to ensure rebirth in a sanctified life." This new life is "made *real* (Eliade's italics) by the incorporation of the sacred." The yogin symbolism of death and rebirth is one of "death to the profane human condition" (p. 362). Elsewhere, he states: "Death prepares the new, purely spiritual birth, access to a mode of living not subject to the destroying action of Time" (*Birth and Rebirth,* New York: 1938, p. 136). This is in keeping

with his study of initiation ceremonies in archaic societies, in which he finds that death signifies a passing from the profane to the sacred (*The Sacred and the Profane*, pp. 191-192). In Altizer's study of Eliade, he writes that for Eliade, "a return to the sacred is effected by the reversal of life, by annihilation of the profane, in short, by an experience of death." Thomas Altizer, *Mircea Eliade and the Dialectic of the Sacred* (Philadelphia: 1963), p. 94.

For an earlier anthropologist's view of the sacred, see Arnold van Gennep, *The Rites of Passage* (1908: reprinted Chicago: 1960), p. ix, and pp. 146-147. See also Karl Rahner, *On the Theology of Death*, p. 71.

With all this, it should again be stressed that in Judaic thought it is life which is sacred: biblical and post-biblical attitudes emphasize *hayim*— "life"—as one of the greatest goods, as noted above. And although R. Meir is reported to have written on the margin of his Bible that Genesis 1:31 ("and it was very good") actually refers to death because death takes man to a sinless world where there is no Evil Inclination (*yezer hara'*; see, Midrash Rabbah Genesis 9), the overwhelming rabbinic sentiment is that a life of serving the Lord is this world is better than life in the world to come in which there can be no such service. See, Mishnah 'Abot 4:22.

247. In a statement somewhat reminiscent of this, Heidegger says that death is "anticipated each moment of my life, in my very act of living." (Cited in Martin-Achard, *Death to Life*, p. 19, n. 20). Martin-Achard himself describes death as taking place when the Divine withdraws and death, always present, comes to the fore. See also, J. M. Demske, *A Key to Heidegger*, p. 110, on this theme.

248. From an ancient Samaritan song cited in JPOS XIX (1939), p. 200.

249. Although it is outside the purview of this study, this suggests that the purpose of evil, represented by *tum'ah*, is that it is to be overcome. On the general theme of *tum'ah*'s mystical relationship to purity, see R. Alshikh's (sixteenth century) commentary on Ruth 3:2.

250. Cited in *Shem Mishmuel* Leviticus p. 324, col. a. Elsewhere, the *Zohar* states that "the spirit of *tum'ah* . . . is wont to hover over an emptied out place." See Zohar's comment on *Sidrah Jethro*, at 67a.

251. Mishnah Yadaim 4:6.

252. See, readings in *Interpreter's Bible* VI, pp. 914-915.

253. See, Brown, Driver, and Briggs, *A Hebrew and English Lexicon of*

the Old Testament (Boston, 1907), p. 380, *"tam'ah,"* concerning the difficulty of this passage.

254. The conceptual root for *tamé* as strange or alien may derive simply from the concept that a foreign land has less sanctity and is in this sense "defiled." For additional examples of alternative readings of *tamé,* see above, p. 53.

255. Temurah 32a-32b.

256. See above, pp. 51-52.

257. Letter dated Baltimore, Md., December 15, 1969. On the subject of basing theologies on word-studies see the important work of James Barr, *The Semantics of Biblical Language* (London: Oxford Univ. Press, (1961) p. 107: "The past of a word is no infallible guide to its present meaning." Barr sounds cautionary notes about the over-use of etymology here, and in his "Etymology and the Old Testament," *Oudtestamentische Studien* XIX (Leiden: E. J. Brill: 1974), pp. 1-28. See also, his "Common Sense and Biblical Language," *Biblica* XLIX (1968) pp. 377-387.

258. For more on the thirst of the dead, see A. Parrot, *Le "Refrigerium" dans l'au-dela,* (Paris: 1937), cited in Edmond Jacob, *Theology of the Old Testament,* p. 305, n. 3.

259. Gaster, *Thespis,* pp. 203 ff.; see also, T. Canaan, "Mohammedan Saints and Sanctuaries in Palestine," *JPOS* 4 (1924), p. 27, which recounts modern Palestinian beliefs concerning souls which revisit the tomb on Friday nights for water. See also, Isaiah 5:13, which refers to a thirst of the dead.

260. Brown, Driver, Briggs, p. 380, derive this form from the Aramaic *tamem,* a stopping up of the ear or heart, and the Arabic "fill, or choke up"; see also, the Lexicon of Gesenius (1854), p. 366, on Job 18:3, " 'stupid in your eyes' is better than 'defiled in your eyes.' " That is to say, a violation of the holiness code will "stop up" the connection and attachment between you and God: *tum'ah,* again, is estrangement.

261. Yoma 39a.

262. Yalqut Shimoni, Proverbs, 943. See also, R. Haim HaKohen's view cited in Tosafists on Ketubot 103b.

SECTION II

1. J. Moed Qatan 3, 5; Chavel, *Commandments,* I, p. 48; Zebaḥim 100b. For biblical allusions to the seven-day period, see I Samuel 31:13, I Chronicles 10:12. See also, Judith 16:24; Ecclesiasticus 22:12. The

practice of Job's three friends, who "sit with him on the ground seven days and seven nights" (Job 2:13), is connected with the rites of mourning.

2. See, Maimonides, *Mishneh Torah*, "Law of Mourning," 1:1, and discussion, *ad loc.* See also, Maimonides, Commandment 37, p. 47: "On this commandment (Leviticus 10:19) is based the duty of mourning"; and p. 48: "Even a priest is bound to observe mourning on the first day." Zebaḥim 100b considers only the first day of mourning to be Scripturally binding. See also, J. Pesaḥim 8:8, and 82b; J. Moed Qatan 3:5.

3. Moed Qatan 20a.

4. Genesis Rabbah 14; J. Berakhot 3:5.

5. The first three days of mourning are somewhat more severe in their requirements than the balance of the first week.

6. See, Zebaḥim 100b.

7. J. Berakhot 3:1.

8. Berakhot 17b; for an English language discussion, see, *Code of Hebrew Law: Yoreh De'ah,* transl. by C. N. Denburg (Montreal: 1954), 341:1, p. 58.

9. Horayot 12b; Maimonides, *"Laws of Entrance into the Sanctuary,"* 2:8; *Yalqut Shimoni* 533; see also, Hosea 9:4: *k'leḥem onim,* "as the bread of mourners."

10. Leviticus 10:16-20; Horayot 12b; Maimonides, "The Sanctuary," 2:7 ff. Contrast this with the story of Xenophon who, when he hears that his son is dead, stops and removes the garlands from his head even though he is in the midst of sacrificing. But he decides that the glorious death of his son is not a cause for lamentation and resumes the sacrifice. Cited in Lieberman, "After-life in Early Rabbinic Literature," p. 164, n. 4.

11. Deuteronomy 26:14; Bikkurim 2:2.

12. Berakhot 3:1; *Yoreh De'ah* 341:1.

13. Moed Qatan 27b; this refers specifically to the first meal after burial.

14. Baba Bathra 16a; J. Moed Qatan 3:8, 9.

15. See, Tosefta Moed Qatan 2:17, Sotah 35a; and see, Lieberman "After-Life in Early Rabbinic Literature," pp. 511 ff., for a full discussion of these sources. Lieberman also cites what he considers a lost Midrash manuscript that refers to "the Amorites [who] were at that moment eating at the grave of Job." See also, Gedalyahu Allon's essay, "On the Source of an Ancient Burial Custom in Israel," (Hebrew) in his *Meḥqarim* II, pp. 99-105, especially pp. 103 ff., for a discussion of food for the dead.

16. "The meal of comfort," or literally, "the meal of restoration."

17. See also, Deuteronomy 26:14; Hosea 9:4; Ezekiel 24:22.

18. Baba Bathra 16a.

19. J. Berakhot 3, 1.

20. See, Maimonides, *Mishneh Torah*, "Laws of Mourning," 4:6-7. In Joel 2:12, fasting, weeping, and mourning are all placed in apposition.

21. II Samuel 3:35.

22. A. E. Cowley, *Aramaic Papyri* (Oxford: 1923), p. 112, lines 15 ff. For funeral meals in other societies, see Goody, *Death, Property, and the Ancestors* pp. 198 ff.; Edwin O. James, *Sacrifice and Sacrament* (London: 1962), pp. 161, 294; H. Helbaek, "Vegetables in the Funeral Meals of Pre-Urban Rome," in *Acta Instituti romani regni Sueciae*, Series 4, 17, pp. 287-294. Although meals for dead ancestors are quite common, there is no biblical evidence for leaving food for the dead as a sacrificial meal for the ancestors, according to Walther Eichrodt, *Theology of the Old Testament*, II, p. 217.

For a discussion of the role of fasting in early Judaism, see J. A. Montgomery, *"Ascetic Strains in Early Judaism,"* in JBL 51 (1932), 187 ff., in which various types of fasts are discussed: positive fasts, mourning fasts, fasts for illumination, public fasts.

23. Moed Qatan 14b, 18a; Semaḥot 7:11; cf. I Samuel 4:12; Isaiah 15:2; 22:12; Jeremiah 41:5; Micah 1:16. See below, pp. 147 ff., for a discussion of the exegetical methods employed by the Rabbis. See, Jan Zandee, *Death as an Enemy in Ancient Egyptian Conceptions,* (Leiden: 1960), p. 207, for a discussion of hair as a token of mourning in Egypt.

24. Moed Qatan 15.

25. See, II Samuel 14:2: " . . . mourn . . . do not anoint with oil . . ."; and Isaiah 61:3: " . . . oil of joy in place of mourning. . . ."

26. Moed Qatan 15b; 23a.

27. Ibid., 15b, 20b; see also, II Samuel 15:30.

28. See, Moed Qatan 15b, 15a, 21a, (and 28b according to the reading of Maimonides), for the sources of these practices.

29. Moed Qatan 15b, with the reading of Rashi; see, J. Moed Qatan 3:5; and J. Berakhot 3:1; "Bar Kappara says, A beautiful image did I have in your house, and you caused me to upset it; so also must you upset your bed." J. Berakhot 3:1 offers another reason: "Why does he sleep in an overturned bed? So that he should be awake all night and be reminded that he is a mourner." It is important to note, incidentally, that

the concept of *death as affecting the divine image in man* is a key concept in the laws of mourning.

30. See also II Samuel 15:30; Jeremiah 14:4; Esther 6:12.

31. Moed Qatan 15a.

32. See, Maimonides, *Mishneh Torah*, "Laws of Entering the Sanctuary," 2:11. For discussions on the significance of the number seven in mourning rites, see A. Kapelrud, "The Number Seven in Ugaritic Texts," *VT* 18 (1968), p. 495 f., who points to seven as the number of completeness, of fate, indefiniteness, danger, intensity; see also E. C. Kingsbury, "A Seven Day Ritual in the Old Babylonian Cult at Larsa," *HUCA* 34 (1963), pp. 1-34; on the role of seven and other numbers in the Judaic tradition, see Yitzhak Heinemann, *Ta'ame ha-Mitzvot*, I p. 68 f.; see also, M. D. A. Cassuto, "Biblical Literature and Canaanite Literature," (Hebrew), *Tarbiẓ* 13, (1942), pp. 197-212, esp. 206-207. The number seventy is also of special significance, as in Naḥmanides' discussion of Numbers 11:16, "Gather unto Me seventy men. . . ." He refers to seventy as the "complete number" (*mispar hashalem*). See Chavel, *Commentary of Naḥmanides* II, pp. 243-244.

33. Semaḥot 7:8, 9.

34. Moed Qatan 23a; Semaḥot 10:12. Perhaps in this last requirement we have another indication of the mourner's estrangement from God. He changes his usual seat in the synagogue because his relationship with Him has been disturbed by the incursion of death into life. He must, according to some authorities, change to a location in the synagogue farther away from the Holy Ark. See, Moed Qatan 23a; Semaḥot 10:12; *Yoreh De'ah*, 393:2.

35. Moed Qatan 20b.

36. See Yebamot 22b, in which the wife is accorded the same status as a blood relative.

37. Moed Qatan 25b.

38. See, Semaḥot 20: "We mourn for the suicide only to the extent that it is in the honor of the living to do so." For a good summary of attitudes towards suicide, see Fred Rosner, "Suicide in Biblical, Talmudic, and Rabbinic Writings," *Tradition* 11 (Summer, 1970), pp. 25-40. See also, Leon Nemoy, "Suicide According to Old Testament Law," *JBL* 57 (1938), pp. 412 ff.; and Wächter, *Tod im Alten Testament*, pp. 89 ff.

39. J. Moed Qatan 3:5.

40. Moed Qatan 19a.

41. Ibid., 14b.

42. Ibid., 19a; 14b; Tosefta Moed Qatan 2.

43. These views are summarized in Lods, *Israel,* p. 225, and in Martin-Achard, *Death to Life,* pp. 25 ff. See our discussion above, pp. 9-16.

44. For a perceptive anthropological view of primitive mourning rites, see van Gennep, *Rites of Passage,* pp. 146-47.

45. Maurice Lamm, *The Jewish Way in Death and Mourning* (New York: 1969), in an excellent factual presentation, occasionally reverts to "psychologizing" the rites, as on pp. 77 ff. Simon Noveck, ed., *Judaism and Psychiatry* (New York: 1956), pp. 105 ff. is another example of this approach, as are the two articles by I. W. Kidorf, "Jewish Tradition and the Freudian Theory of Mourning", and "The Shiva: a Form of Group Psychotherapy," *Journal of Religion and Health* 2 (1962-1963), pp. 248-252; and 5 (1966), pp. 43-47.

46. Bronislav Malinowsky, *Magic, Science, and Religion* (New York: 1954), pp. 42-53.

47. Genesis Rabbah 8:11.

48. This goes somewhat beyond Pedersen's view of Israelite mourning practice, in which the mourning family is aware of the discord in its life, and places itself outside the normal life, as is true "in all cases where people are brought face to face with unhappiness and sorrow" which removes man from normal community. See, Johannes Pedersen, *Israel: Its Life and Culture* (Copenhagen: 1954), I-II, pp. 494 ff. Pedersen is extremely sensitive to the profound issue of mourning, although he does not discuss the role of *tum'ah* in our context. He does state that the mourner "is in the world of uncleanness and curse," but this is in the terms of what, for Pedersen, are the humbling effects of death.

49. In a particularly poignant exegesis of Genesis 9:2, Shabbat 151b expresses the end of man's dominion over nature when he dies:

> As long as man is alive, his fear lies upon dumb creatures (Genesis 9:2); once he dies, this fear ceases. Therefore, even a mighty man like Og, King of Bashan (the prototype of physical strength) needs guarding once he dies, for fear of weasels and mice who may gnaw at him. But a day-old infant, alive, need not be guarded.

G. von Rad refers to death as "a diminished form of human existence." Von Rad, *Theology,* I, p. 369.

50. Taanit 17a; Sanhedrin 22b. See Maimonides, "Entering the Sanctuary," I: 8-14, where untended, overgrown hair is a manifestation of *nivul,* personal degradation.

51. Shabbat 113a.

52. On the subject of shoes as symbols of man's dignity, see also Shabbat 129a and Rashi, *ad loc.*; Shabbat 114a; Berakhot 43b; Pesaḥim 112a, 113b; Yoma 78b; Ketubot 64b, 65b. The surviving brother who refuses to fulfill his levirate marriage obligations to the widow of his brother must undergo a *ḥalizah* ceremony (Deuteronomy 25:5-11; Yebamot 12:1). As part of the rites, the widow "comes nigh unto him in the presence of the elders, and pulls his shoe from off his foot." See Ruth 4: 6-8. In the light of the significance of the shoe it is possible that the removal of the shoe is an attempt to strip him, at least symbolically, of his dignity as a man, since he has refused to take on the obligation of levirate marriage, i.e., to carry on the life force of his brother (*l'haqim shem*).

53. Particularly during the first three days of mourning.

54. See also Mishnah Abot 6:7, where Torah is equated with life. See Exodus Rabbah 51:8: " 'Engraved—*ḥarut*—on the tablets' (Exodus 32:16), R. Neḥemia says, "Read rather '*ḥerut*—'free'—free from the Angel of Death"; that is, Torah frees from death. See also, *ibid.*, 33.

55. Moed Qatan 15b.

56. J. Moed Qatan 3:5; Moed Qatan 15b; Dov Zlotnick, *Tractate Mourning* (New Haven: 1966), p. 112, n. 60; see also above p. 86, for discussion of overturning the bed.

On the general subject of sexual abstinence during mourning, see Norman Brown, *Life Against Death* (New York: 1957), pp. 112 ff.; van Gennep, *Rites,* p. 169: He who has entered the "sacred" world of death must put himself in a condition of "purity." Effie Bendan, *Death Customs,* p. 133, 235 f., and H. Kelsen, *Society and Nature* (London: 1946), pp. 163-164: To the primitives there is a connection between the sex act and death, and one may die during procreation unless there are proper safeguards. Lods, *Israel,* p. 271: The spirits of the act of birth should have no contact with the spirits of the dead.

That the sex act may have been the first cause of death in the world is alluded to in several rabbinic sources which maintain that Adam's sin was connected with the sex act. See Genesis Rabbah 18:6; Canticles Rabbah 4:4; Shabbat 145b; Abodah Zarah 22b; Yebamot 103b.

57. Baba Bathra 16b: "Why are lentils proper food for mourners?. As the lentils roll, so does mourning roll from one person to the next. As the lentil is silent without a cleft opening, so is the mourner silent." Eggs are also mentioned as a proper mourning food for the same reason.

58. For a contemporary discussion, within a different context, of the

community aspects of the word *shalom,* see Eugene C. Bianchi, *Reconciliation* (New York: 1969), p. 7.

59. See also, Judges 6:24: "God *Shalom.* . . ."

60. See Denburg, *Yoreh De'ah,* p. 300, n. 11, for an English language discussion of greeting of the mourner and *shalom.*

61. Ibid., par. 390, pp. 316 ff., contains a full listing of the acts of body care prohibited to the mourner.

62. See above, pp. 81-82.

63. There is an interruption of mourning on a festival as well, should it occur during the seven-day period, as noted above, p. 88.

64. See, Maimonides, *Guide of the Perplexed,* II:31, p. 359: ". . . we are ordered by the Law to exalt this day in order that the principle of the creation of the world in time be established and universally known [because it is written] 'For in six days. . . .'" See also, Soferim 13,14: "the Sabbath was created before Israel," when the world was created.

65. Berakhot 57b, and numerous other sources in Talmudic and Midrashic literature.

66. Mekhilta to Exodus 31:17; Rosh Hashanah 31a. See, Abraham Joshua Heschel, *The Sabbath* (New York: 1951), pp. 72-78, for a discussion on this theme. Heschel cites *Vita Adae et Evae,* 41.1, *The Apocrypha and Pseudepigrapha,* ed., Charles, II, 151: "The seventh day is the sign of resurrection and the world to come."

67. See, the numerous biblical references to God sanctifying (*meqadesh*) the Sabbath, and numerous rabbinic allusions similar to *Seder Eliyahu Rabbah,* ed., M. Friedman (Vienna: 1902), p. 133: "The holiness of the Lord, the holiness of the Sabbath, the holiness of Israel, are all like one." See also, Nedarim 78b: The Sabbath, unlike festivals, does not need sanctification by the rabbinic courts, since it is already sanctified.

68. The Talmud may be making an oblique reference to the inability of God and death to dwell together when it states: "For a day-old infant the Sabbath is desecrated; for David King of Israel, dead, the Sabbath must not be desecrated" (Shabbat 151b). On the Sabbath, the holy day of God, a corpse may not be touched—even by a lay Israelite. The Rabbis prohibit closing the eyes of a corpse on the Sabbath.

69. See Psalms 22:3, 39:3, 94:17, for *dmm* as "still, motionless." The passage in Psalms 4:5 is read by Berakhot 5a as a reference to death.

70. For example, Mitchell Dahood, "Textual Problems in Isaiah," *CBQ* 22 (1960), 400 ff.

71. Mitchell Dahood, "Philological Studies in Lamentations," *Biblica*

49 (1968): p. 38 f. See also, review by Godfrey Rolles Driver, in JSS 5, (1960). 157, which discusses the Accadian *damamu as* "moan." See also, the suggestive rabbinic text in Shabbat 152b, in which *duma* is the name of the guardian angel of the deceased. According to Midrash Shoḥer Tov 11, *duma* guides the spirits out of Hades each night, and the spirits eat and drink in the area called *chatzar mavet,* "in complete silence." See also, Abodah Zarah 20b. It is very likely that *duma* is the personification of *silence.*

72. Dahood, "Problems in Isaiah." p. 402.

73. See Baba Bathra 16b; J. Berakhot 3, 1; see discussions above, note 57.

74. See pp. 63-72.

75. P. 81. Cf. also the Midrashic remark, "In the world to come, the Holy One will overturn mourning into joy, as it is written (Jer. 31:12), 'And I will turn their mourning (*eblam*) into joy.'" Jeremiah and Amos are each focusing on similar themes: the opposite of *ebel.*

76. Robert Graves and Raphael Patai, *Hebrew Myths* (London: 1964), p. 274.

77. For a full discussion of the "threshing floor" in rites of mourning, see A. J. Wensinck, *Some Semitic Rites of Mourning and Religion.* (Amsterdam: 1917), Chapter I. See also, Hvidberg, *Weeping and Laughter,* p. 106.

78. Van de Leeuw, *Religion in Essence and Manifestation,* p. 200.

79. Ibid., p. 199.

80. See earlier discussion, p. 86, concerning Ezekiel 24:17, "Bind they headtire upon thee." Moed Qatan 15a takes this to refer to phylacteries, which only Ezekiel is commanded to wear since he is a priest, but which others in deep mourning may not wear.

81. Semaḥot 6:3.

82. Ibid., citing Ketubot 8b; see also, J. Ketubot 1, 1.

83. Soferim 19,12; Pirkei d'R. Eleazer 17; Zlotnick, Semaḥot, p. 126, n. 12; literally, the citation reads that the people would "offer *ḥesed* one to the other."

84. Ketubot 17a.

85. Midrash Rabbah Genesis, 63:14.

86. Midrash Rabbah Genesis, 27:4.

87. See above p. 85 based on Moed Qatan 15b; and above p. 95, concerning "turn over the middle-man."

88. Shabbat 87a; Bezah 5b.

89. J. Berakhot 3:4; Berakhot 22a.

90. Moed Qatan 14-16.

91. In this connection it is pertinent to note that there have been a number of modern attempts to "coincide opposites." Rilke, Heidegger, and Dostoevski are usually cited as the chief proponents of drawing "the beyond into the here and now," of reaching "eternity through total immersion of time," of eternity becoming time. See Thomas J. J. Altizer, *Mircea Eliade and the Dialetic of the Sacred* (Philadelphia: 1963), pp. 92-93, and p. 113. In a different context Martin-Achard, *From Death to Life*, p. 16, points out that Old Testament psychology can accept contradictions which, to us, are mutually exclusive.

92. Denburg, *Code* 334:2, and *B'er Hagolah, ad loc.*, which bases this requirement on the story of Hyrcanus in Sanhedrin 68a, and on Moed Qatan 15b.

93. Unlike the mourner he may study in private.

94. Baba Mezia 59b; see Tosafot, *ad loc.,* 95 Baba Mezia 59b; on mourning clothes, see Genesis 38:14, "the clothes of widowhood," and II Samuel 1:2, "and wear the clothes of mourning."

95. Baba Mezia 59b.

96. He is different from the mourner in two details: unlike the mourner he remains under ban even during a festival; and, on ordinary weekdays, the excommunicant may work.

97. See above, p. 101.

98. See Zlotnick, *Semahot*, p. 126, n. 12.

99. See Zebahim 6:3; J. Succah, 5:8, -55d.

100. The mourner is offered condolences, while the excommunicant is offered the hope that he will soon be restored to full favor with "Him Who dwells in this house."

101. See Soncino edition of Talmud Berakhot, p. 108, n. 3.

102. Berakhot, 18a; Semahot 13.

103. Berakhot 3b; 18a.

104. Midrash Rabbah Genesis 96, p. 927; Midrash Rabbah Ecclesiastes 7, 2:5.

105. Hedwig Jahnow's seminal study is perhaps the classic statement on this subject. See her, "Das Hebräische Leichenlied im Rahmen der Völkerdichtung", *BZAW* 36 (1923). Important contributions have also been made by Karl Budde, "Das Hebräische Klagelied," *ZAW* 2 (1882) pp. 1-52; and by Paul Kahle, "Die Totenklage im Heutigen Aegypten," in *Eucharisterion* (H. Gunkel Festschrift: Gottingen: 1923), I, pp. 346-

399. See also N. K. Gottwald, *Studies in the Book of Lamentations* (Chicago: 1954), esp. pp. 34-47; and H. J. Elhorst, "Die israelitischen Trauerriten," in *Wellhausen Presentation Volume,* ed., Karl Marti (Giessen: 1914), pp. 117-128, esp. pp. 120-121.

106. All translations and notes are from the Soncino Press edition of the Talmud. Those by the author are indicated by the initials "E.F." In addition, the laments have been given their verse form by the author.

For reference purposes, the individual laments have been given Roman numerals. These numerals have no other significance.

107. I have no one to answer my questions.

108: Holy Ark: metaphor for Rabbi.

109. Possibly a reference to the mourning rite in which the mourner does not prepare his own food; or a reference to fasting. (E.F.) See R. Hananel, *al loc.: habila* refers to a pledge coming due.

110. In order to wash the dead before burial. This is possibly a reference to the mourner's food restrictions. See, Moed Qatan 23b, Berakhot 17b, Semahot 10:3.

111. *Antikhi* are caldron-like vessels suspended between heated bricks. Perhaps this is a reference to washing the dead before burial. But see Rashi and R. Hananel, *ad loc.*

112. The best wool; according to Rashi, death is as beautiful as a Milesian robe. This may also refer to the making of the shrouds.

113. According to Shabbat 30a, which bases itself on Psalms 88:6, a dead man is "free of Torah and *mitzvot.*" See also, Shabbat 151b.

114. See Numbers 5, 22, concerning the ordeal by water, administered to a wife suspected of adultery.

115. "Gracious," *hnn,* is a play on the father's name, *Honin.*

116. From the context, it is possible that this may not be a lament at all, but an accurate and prosaic statement of legal fact on which basis the "rider's" widow was permitted to remarry.

117. See Jeremiah 25.26.

118. Tiberias.

119. Israel: Jeremiah 31.1.

120. Babylon, which is low.

121. This and the following lament were recited for heathens or slaves.

122. Berakhot 16b cites a variant: "For a faithful servant: Alas, O good and faithful man/who enjoyed his labor."

123. Lament for a suicide.

124. See Psalms 92: "The righteous shall flourish like a palm . . ."

125. See E. Gerstenberger, "The Woe Oracles of the Prophets," JBL 81 (1962), 249 ff., for a discussion of *hoi* and *'oi* in the Bible, and the varying types of statements—threats, forecast of catastrophe, laments, foreboding, indictment—which these terms may introduce. See also, Jahnow, *"Das Hebraische Leichenlied,"* pp. 83-87 on the *hoi* form; and P. Humbert, *Problemes du livre d'Habacuc* (Neuchatel: 1944), pp. 18 ff., for classification of woe words.

126. For a translation of *hoy* as "alas," and not as "woe to," see G. Wanke, *ZAW* 78, (1966), 215-218; R. Clifford, *CBO* 28, (1966), 458-464; W. Janzen, *HTR* 58 (1965), 221; G. E. Wright, *Encounter* 26 (1965), 234; see also H. W. Wolff, *Amos' Geistige Heimat* (Neukirchen: 1964), pp. 12-24.

127. "In Jerusalem, only the actual works of the dead were recited before his bier," Semaḥot 3.6.

128. It is significant that rabbinic prayer for the dead—known as the *qaddish*—recited at the graveside after burial, makes clear reference to God but does not use any specific divine name. Instead it utilizes the phrase *shme rabba,* "His great name," which is to be "exalted and magnified and blessed." But see Tosafists to Berakhot 3a.

129. Ketubot 104a.

130. Sanhedrin 11a; Sotah 48b.

131. For discussions of the significance of names in the Bible, see essay by Otto Eissfeldt, "Renaming in the Old Testament," in *Words and Meaning, Essays Presented to D. W. Thomas,* ed. by P. R. Ackroyd and B. Lindars (Cambridge: 1968), pp. 69-79; Graves and Patai, *Hebrew Myths* (London: 1964), pp. 165, 230; Pedersen, *Israel,* I-II, pp. 245-59; Lods, *Israel,* p. 273. See also Freud, *Totem and Taboo,* p. 145; and Geoffrey Wagner, *On the Wisdom of Words* (Princeton: 1968), pp. 185 ff.

132. The magical properties of names among primitives depended in great measure on the proper rhythmic intonation of the name. Death could be caused by removing a man's name and linking it with some substance which was then destroyed. Cf. J. W. Wevers, "Form Criticism of Individual Complaint Psalms," VT 6 (1956), pp. 82-3.

133. E. B. Taylor, *Researches in the Early History of Mankind,* ed., Paul Bohannan (Chicago: 1964), pp. 119-20.

134. Claude Levi-Strauss, *The Savage Mind* (Chicago: 1966), p. 183.

135. Jørgen Ruud, *Taboo* (Oslo: 1960), p. 171.

136. Effie Bendan, *Death Customs* (New York: 1930), p. 237.

137. Ibid., p. 136; cf. A. P. Elkin, *The Australian Aborigines* (London: 1956), p. 302. For interesting analyses of name taboos, see C. Levi-Strauss, *The Savage Mind*, pp. 191-216, and Lucien Levy-Bruhl, *The Soul of the Primitive*, (New York: 1928), pp. 208, 326 ff.

138. Pp. 13 ff.

139. In general, rabbinic interest in names is very great. Cf. Leviticus Rabbah 32:5 about changing names. Certain Talmudic sages were known as "name interpreters" (lit., *dorshe shemoth*). Cf. Genesis Rabbah 42:8; Ruth Rabbah 2; Yoma 83b. See Tzvi Kaplan, *B'Halakhah v'Agadah* (Jerusalem: 1959), pp. 58-141, for a thorough discussion of rabbinic interpretation of names.

140. Moed Qatan 8a; 28b; J. Berakhot 3.1; and other sources.

141. An Aramaic funeral lament is found on Jason's tomb, using the words *quina 'alma* "a powerful lament." It appeals to all to lament over Jason; a divine appeal to Jason wishes him peace in the tomb; and it expresses the sorrow of Jason's friends. Cf. N. Avigad, "Aramaic Inscriptions in the Tomb of Jason," *IEJ* 17 (1967), p. 103. Note also that the Qaddish prayer, recited at the graveside after burial, is in Aramaic. See Tosafists to Berakhot 3a, for a discussion on the use of Aramaic for the Qaddish: "everyone (the non-scholars) understood it (Aramaic) for this was their tongue."

It should be noted that the laments from M.Q. 28b (numbers VII-XIII) are in all likelihood examples of the type of muted laments which would be chanted on *ḥol-hamoed,* the Intermediate Days of a festival, as is evident from the context in M.Q. It is also conceivable that these examples are merely extant fragments of longer laments.

142. Baba Meẓia 86a. According to some interpreters, the upheaval in the laws of nature, indicated in these examples, is a sign of divine wrath at the death of His righteous men. See Soncino Baba Meẓia p. 496.

The personification of inanimate objects is a common feature of the biblical lament, according to Jahnow, "Das hebraische Leichenlied," pp. 102-103. One can only speculate as to why. Now that death is seen at first hand, does the mourner—perhaps in spite of death—ascribe life to everything, even to inanimate objects? Is this a poignant example of his attachment to the quality of livingness? Is he saying that nothing is—or wishing that nothing were—dead—not the inanimate object, and not his dead loved one? Or is it simply the usual apostrophe not uncommon at moments of intense emotion?

143. Shabbat 105b.

144. Hvidberg, *Weeping and Laughter,* p. 56.

145. Midrash Rabbah Genesis 100.2.

146. Moed Qatan 4.3.

147. Moed Qatan 26b (Italics added.) On the efficacy of weeping, see Ber. 32b; Sanh. 104b; Rosh Hashanah 18a, 34a.

148. MQ 27b.

149. Sem. 8:7.

150. Saul Lieberman, "After-Life in Early Rabbinic Literature," in *H. A. Wolfson Jubilee Volume* II (Jerusalem: 1965), p. 509. Sem. 9:3 refers to those who "rescue vessels" from the dead as "robbers of the dead."

For fuller discussion of objects buried with the dead in post-biblical times, see M. Dothan, "Excavations at Horvat Beter (Beersheba)" *'Atiqot* 2 (1959), pp. 18-19, concerning cooking pans found in graves; J. J. Rothschild, "The Tombs of Sanhedria," PEQ 84 (1952) p. 24, which discusses burying the dead in garments they wore when alive; B. Mazar, *Beth Shearim* (Jerusalem: 1957), pp. 143, 150, discussing women's eye-paint; Josephus, *Ant.* 13:8:4; Tobit 4:11, which indicates that food offerings may have been utilized as late as the second century. Sanh. 48a-b refers to throwing of clothes on the dead as an act of mourning, but cf. MR Ecclesiastes 2:24.

For a discussion of the differences between magical weeping and ritual mourning, see T. Gaster, *Thespis, op. cit.,* pp. 32-34.

151. Cf. B. Long, "The Divine Funeral Lament," JBL 85 (1966), p. 85, for a full discussion of divine laments in Akkadian and Ugaritic, as well as in the Bible; and cf. ANET p. 108a, lines 5 ff., and 139b, as pointed out by Jahnow.

152. Shabb. 105b.

153. MQ 27b.

154. Sem. 3:6.

155. Ned. 40a.

156. Shabb. 21b.

157. See also Sem. 14:7.

158. ANET, p. 109a, lines 49 ff.

159. Th. Gaster, *Thespis* (New York, 1961), p. 31.

160. G. Rachel-Levy, *Religious Conceptions of the Stone Age* (New York, 1963), p. 235.

161. Cited in E. O. James, *The Tree of Life, op. cit.,* p. 224, which discusses other theories as well.

162. Stephen Langdon, *Babylonian Liturgies* (Paris: 1913), pp. xxix ff.

163. S. B. Finesinger, "Musical Instruments in the Old Testament," HUCA (1926), pp. 48-52.

164. K. Meyer-Baer, *Music of the Spheres and the Dance of Death* (Princeton: 1970), pp. 226 ff.

165. Cf. G. Van der Leeuw, *Sacred and Profane Beauty* (New York: 1963), p. 214 for further discussion on the significance of the flute in religion.

166. See also I K. 13:29; II Sam. 3:33-4; 13:36; Jer. 16:5-6; Ez. 24:23; 27:30; 28:32; II Chr. 35:25; Ben Sirah 38:16-17.

167. MQ 8a; Nedarim 666; Kethubot 4:4.

168. Wailing was to stop once burial actually took place. 3:9. Mishnah Oholoth discusses the "field of mourning."

The question of when precisely eulogies were actually delivered is discussed by L. Finkelstein, *The Pharisees* (Philadelphia: 1938), V. I p. 48. The eulogies by residents of Jerusalem were cautious and without exaggeration, as in Sem. 3:6. In the Galilee and Jerusalem, it was customary to recite eulogies before the funeral, at the deceased's house; in Judean villages it was done after the funeral. Finkelstein's largely economic thesis that certain aristocrats developed funeral practices opposed to those of the poor peasantry of the Galilee has been vigorously disputed by numerous scholars including W. F. Albright in a lecture heard by this author in Baltimore, 1950.

169. For a discussion of special places for mourning rites, see A. J. Wensinck, *Some Semitic Rites of Mourning and Religion* (Amsterdam: 1917), pp. 1-11.

170. Th. Gaster, *Thespis,* p. 52, n. 74, and p. 78. For a full discussion of cultic weeping, see F. F. Hvidberg, *Weeping and Laughter in the Old Testament,* pp. 98-137.

171. Cf. C. J. Bleeker, *The Sacred Bridge* (Leiden: 1963), p. 190.

172. John A. Wilson, "Funeral Services in the Egyptian Old Kingdom," JNES 3 (1944), pp. 203-204.

173. J. Zandee, *Death As an Enemy According to Ancient Egyptian Conceptions* (Leiden: 1960), p. 45.

174. Mircea Eliade, "Australian Religions: Death, Eschatology, and Some Conclusions," *Journal of Religions* 7 (1967-8), p. 245; cf. also Meir Braverman's essay, "The Etymology of Arabic Ma'tam 'Mourning Assembly' " in *Studies and Essays in Honor of Abraham A. Neuman,* ed. by M. Ben-Horin, B. D. Weinryb, S. Zeitlin, (Leiden: 1962), pp. 88-93, for a discussion of mourning women in the Arab tradition.

175. Raphael Patai, "The Shekhina" *Journal of Religion,* 44 (1964), pp. 284 ff.

176. Lamentations Rabbah, Introduction, 24.

177. Sperling, *Ta'amei HaMinhagim,* p. 441, par. 10032. Professional Jewish wailing women are still prevalent in Baghdad, according to H. I. Zimmels, *Ashkenazim and Sephardim* (London: 1958), p. 183.

178. Berakhoth 51a.

179. Pesiqta Rabbati, 139a.

180. Pritchard, ANET, pp. 18 ff.

181. John A. Wilson in JNES, *op. cit.,* p. 203; A. Sendrey, *Music in Ancient Israel* (New York: 1969), p. 479; Hastings, *Encyclopedia of Religion and Ethics,* X, p. 359b.

182. Meyer-Baer, pp. 226 ff.

183 I K. 17-18: the limping dances around the altar with laments to Baal.

184 G. Scholem, *Major Trends in Jewish Mysticism* (New York: 1954), p. 153.

185. Abraham Sabba, *Tzeror Hamor,* (Venice: c. 1576); for a full discussion of the role of the dance in death, see G. Van der Leeuw, *Sacred and Profane Beauty,* pp. 43 ff.

186. MQ 3:9.

187. Keth. 4:4 and 48a; Mishnah BM 8:1.

188. For a more detailed discussion of funeral music in rabbinic times, see A. Sendrey, pp. 441-495.

189. MQ 28 a-b.

190. See Robert North, "The Cain Music," JBL 83 (1964), pp. 379, 386 ff., 389, in which he suggests that King David and his musical prowess are descendants of Cain in Genesis, since David was a Kenite. But according to rabbinic understanding of the name "Cain," it stems from *qinyan,* "possession." "Lament" is from *qnn.* Furthermore, David comes from Moab and Judah.

Bibliography

Albright, W. F. *The Archaeology of Palestine*. London, 1960.

Altizer, T. J. J. *Mircea Eliade and the Dialectic of the Sacred*. Philadelphia, 1963.

Anthony, Sylvia. *The Child's Discovery of Death*. London, 1940.

Avigad, N. "Aramaic Inscriptions in the Tomb of Jason." I.E.J. 17 1967, p. 103.

Barr, James. *The Semantics of Biblical Language*. London, 1961

Bendann, Effie. *Death Customs*. New York, 1930.

Berkovits, Eliezer. *Man and God*. Detroit, 1969.

Bettelheim, Bruno. *Symbolic Wounds*. Glencoe, 1954.

Bianchi, E. C. *Reconciliation*. New York, 1969.

Birkeland, Harris. "The Belief in the Resurrection of the Dead in the Old Testament." *Studia Theologica,* 3-4 1949-1950, pp. 60-79.

Bleeker, C. J. *The Sacred Bridge*. Leiden, 1963.

Boman, Thorlief. *Hebrew Thought Compared with Greek*. Philadelphia, 1960.

Borowitz, Eugene B. *A New Jewish Theology in the Making*. Philadelphia, 1968.

Brandon, S. G. F. *Man and His Destiny in the Great Religions*. London, 1962.

———. *The Judgement of the Dead*. New York, 1967.

———. "The Personification of Death in Some Ancient Religions." BJRL 43 1960-61, p. 320.

Braverman, Meir. "The Etymology of Arabic Ma'tam 'Mourning Assembly.'" *Studies and Essays in Honor of Abraham A. Newman,* ed. by M. Ben-Horin, B. D. Weinryb, S. Zeitlin, (Leiden, 1962), pp. 88-93.

Brown, Norman. *Life Against Death*. New York, 1957.

Buchler, A. *Studies in Sin and Atonement in the Rabbinic Literature of the First Century*. (Reprinted New York: Ktav, for Library of Biblical Studies), 1967.

———. "The Levitical Impurity of the Gentiles." JQR n.s. XVII, pp. 1-81.

Budde, Karl. "Das Hebräische Klagelied." ZAW 2 1882, pp. 1-52.

Canaan, T. "Mohammedan Saints and Sanctuaries in Palestine." JPOS 4 1924, p. 27.

Chavel, Charles, trans., Maimonides, *The Book of Commandments*. London, 1957.

Cowley, A. E. *Aramaic Papyri*. Oxford, 1923.

Curtis, J. "The Mount of Olives in the Judaeo-Christian Tradition." HUCA 28 1957, pp. 146-158.

Dahood, Mitchell. "Textual Problems in Isaiah." CBQ 22 1960, pp. 400ff.

———. "Philological Studies in Lamentations." *Biblica* 49 1968, pp. 38ff.

Danby, Herbert. *The Mishnah*. London, 1933.

Daube, David. "Concessions to Sinfulness in Jewish Law." JJS 10 1959, pp. 1-13.

Demske, J. M. *Being, Man, and Death: A Key to Heidegger*. Lexington: University of Kentucky, 1970.

Dothan, M. "Excavations at Horvat Beter (Beer-Sheba)." *'Atiqot'* 2 1959, pp. 18-19.

Douglas, Mary. *Purity and Danger*. New York, 1966.

———. "Deciphering a Meal." *Daedalus, Winter,* 1972 pp. 61-82.

Eichrodt, W. *Theology of the Old Testament*. Philadelphia, 1967.

Eissfeldt, Otto. "Renaming in the Old Testament." *Words and Meaning, Essays Presented to D. W. Thomas,* ed. by P. R. Ackroyd and B. Lindars. Cambridge, 1968, pp. 69-79.

Elhorst, H. J. "Die israelitischen Trauerriten," *Wellhausen Presentation Volume,* ed. Karl Marti. Giessen, 1914, pp. 117-128, esp. 120-121.

Eliade, Mircea. *Yoga, Immortality and Freedom*. New York, 1958.

———. *Birth and Rebirth*. New York, 1958.

———. *The Sacred and the Profane*. New York, 1961.

———. "Australian Religions: Death, Eschatology, and Some Conclusions." *Journal of Religions* 7, 1967-8, p. 245.

Elkin, A. P. *The Australian Aborigines.* London, 1953.

Epstein, Joseph, ed. *A Conspectus of the Public Lectures of* Rabbi Joseph B. Soloveitchik. New York, 1974.

Finesinger, S. B. "Musical Instruments in the Old Testament." HUCA III 1926, pp. 48-52.

Finkelstein, Louis. *The Pharisees.* Philadelphia, 1938.

Frankfort, Henri. *The Birth of Civilization in the Near East.* London, 1951.

Frazer, J. G. *Fear of the Dead in Primitive Religion.* London, 1933.

Freud, Sigmund. *Totem and Taboo.* New York, 1946.

————. *Thoughts for the Times on War and Death: 1915.* New York, 1947.

Gaster, Th. *Thespis: Ritual, Myth, and Drama in the Ancient Near East.* New York, 1961.

Gerstenberger, E. "The Woe Oracles of the Prophets." JBL 81 1962, pp. 249ff.

Goody, Jack. *Death, Property and the Ancestors.* Stanford, 1962.

Gottwald, N. K. *Studies in the Book of Lamentations.* London, 1954.

Graves, Robert and Raphael Patai. *Hebrew Myths.* London, 1964.

Heidel, A. *The Gilgamash Epic and Old Testament Parallels.* Chicago, 1946.

Helbaek, H. "Vegetables in the Funeral Meals of pre-Urban Rome." *Acta Instituti romani regni Sueciae,* Series 4, 17, pp. 287-294.

Heschel, A. J. *The Sabbath.* New York, 1951.

Hirsch, S. R. *Horeb,* transl. I. Grunfeld. London, 1962.

Humbert, P. *Problems du livre d'Habacuc.* Neuchatel, 1944.

Hvidberg, F. F. *Weeping and Laughter.* Leiden, 1962.

Hwa Yol Jung. "The Logic of the Personal: John Macmurray and the Ancient Hebrew View of Life." *The Personalist,* 47 1966, p. 41.

Jacob, E. *Theology of the Old Testament.* New York, 1958.

Jahnow, Hedwig. *Das Hebräische Leichenlied Im Rahmen Der Volkerdichgung.* BZAW 36 1923.

James, E. O. *Comparative Religion.* New York, 1961.

————. *Sacrifice and Sacrament.* London, 1962.

————. *Tree of Life.* Leiden, 1966.

Johnson, A. R. *The Vitality of the Individual.* Cardiff, 1949.

Kahle, Paul. "Die Totenklage im heutigen Ägypten." *Eucharisterion.* H. Gunkel Festschrift: Gottingen, 1923, I, pp. 346-399.

Kapelrud, A. "The Number Seven in Ugaritic Texts." VT 18 1968, pp. 495ff.

Kaufmann, Yehezkel. *The Religion of Israel,* transl. M. Greenberg. Chicago, 1960.

Kelsen, H. *Society and Nature.* London, 1946.

Key, A. A. "The Concept of Death in Early Israelite Religion." HTR 32, pp. 240ff.

Kidorf, I. W. "Jewish Tradition and the Freudian Theory of Mourning." *Journal of Religion and Health* 2 1962-63, pp. 248-252.

————. "The Shiva: a Form of Group Psychotherapy." *Journal of Religion and Health* 5 1966, pp. 43-47.

Kingsbury, E. C. "A Seven Day Ritual in the Old Babylonian Cult at Larsa." HUCA 34 1963, pp. 1-34.

Kramer, Samuel Noah. "Sumero-Akkadian Interconnections: Religious Ideas." *Aspects du Contact Sumero-Akkadien,* Geneva, 1960, pp. 280ff.

Lamm, Maurice. *The Jewish Way in Death and Mourning.* New York, 1969.

Lapp, Paul W. "The Cemetery at Bab edh-Dhra' Jordan." In *Archeological Discoveries in the Holy Land.* New York, 1967, p. 38, pp. 181ff.

————. *A History of the Mishnaic Law of Purities,* Part VI. Leiden, 1975.

Nemoy, Leon. "Suicide According to Old Testament Law." JBL 57 1938, pp. 412ff.

Neusner, Jacob. *The Idea of Purity in Ancient Judaism.* Leiden, 1973.

————. *A History of the Mishnaic Law of Purities,* Part VI, Leiden, 1975.

North, Robert. "The Cain Music." JBL 83 1964, pp. 379, 386ff., 389.

Noveck, Simon, ed. *Great Jewish Thinkers of the Twentieth Century.* Washington, D. C., 1963.

Orlinsky, H. M. *Notes on the New Translation of the Torah.* Philadelphia, 1969.

Otto, Rudolph. *The Idea of the Holy.* London, 1936.

Parrot, A. *Le "Refrigerium" dans l'au-dela.* Paris, 1937.

Patai, Raphael. "The Shekina." *Journal of Religion,* 44 October, 1964, pp. 284ff.

Pedersen, J. *Israel.* Copenhagen, 1954.

Piggot, S. *The Dawn of Civilization.* New York, 1961.

Porten, Bezalel. *Archives from Elephantine.* Berkeley, 1968.

Pritchard, J. B. *Ancient Near Eastern Texts.* Princeton, 1950.

Radcliffe-Brown, A. R. *The Andaman Islanders.* Glencoe, 1948.

Rahmani, L. Y. "Jewish Rock-Cut Tombs in Jerusalem." *'Atiqot* 3, 1961, pp. 117-118.

Rahner, Karl. "Theology of Death." *Modern Catholic Thinkers,* ed. A. R. Caponigri. London, 1960, pp. 152ff.

Ringgren, H. *Faith of Qumran.* Philadelphia, 1963.

————. *Israelite Religion.* Philadelphia, 1966.

Rosner, Fred. "Suicide in Biblical, Talmudic, and Rabbinic Writings." *Tradition* 11-1970, pp. 25-40.

Rothschild, J. "The Tombs of Sanhedria." PEQ 84 1952, pp. 25ff.

Rubenstein, Richard L. *After Auschwitz.* New York, 1966.

Russell, D. S. *The Method and Message of Jewish Apocalyptic.* London, 1964.

Levi-Strauss, Claude. *The Savage Mind.* Chicago, 1966.

Levy-Bruhl, L. *The Soul of the Primitive.* New York, 1928.

————. *Primitives and the Supernatural.* New York, 1935.

Levy, G. Rachel. *Religious Conceptions of the Stone Age.* New York, 1963.

Lieberman, Saul. *Hellenism in Jewish Palestine.* New York, 1950.

————. "After-Life in Early Rabbinic Literature," in *Harry A. Wolfson Jubilee Volume* II New York, 1965, p. 511.

Lods, A. *La Croyance a la vie future dans l'antique Israelite.* Paris, 1906.

————. *Israel.* New York, 1962.

Long, B. "The Divine Funeral Lament." JBL 85 1966.

Lys, Daniel. "The Israelite Soul According to the LXX." VT 16 1966, pp. 181ff.

Macquarrie, John. "True Life in Death." *Journal of Bible and Religion* 31 1963, pp. 204-205.

Malinowsky, B. *Magic, Science and Religion.* New York, 1954.

————. *The Family Among the Australian Aborigines.* New York, 1969.

Martin-Achard, R. *From Death to Life.* Edinburgh, 1960.

Mazar, B. *Beth She'arim.* Jerusalem, 1957.

Meyer-Baer, K. *Music of the Spheres and the Dance of Death.* Princeton, 1970.

Mills, Liston O. *Perspectives on Death.* Nashville, 1969.

Mitchell, T. C. "The Old Testament Usage of *Neshama.*" VT 11 1961, pp. 177-187.

Montgomery, J. A. "Ascetic Strains in Early Judaism." JBL 51 1932, pp. 187ff.

Mowinckel, S. *He That Cometh.* New York, 1954.

Ruud, Jørgen. *Taboo.* Oslo, 1960.

Sanders, J. A. *Dead Sea Psalm Scrolls.* Ithaca, 1967.

Scholem, G. *Major Trends in Jewish Mysticism.* New York, 1954.

Schwarzbaum, Haim. "Jewish, Christian, Moslem and Falasha Legends of the Death of Aaron, the High Priest." *Fabula* 5-6, 1962, p. 192.

Sendrey, A. *Music in Ancient Israel.* New York, 1969.

Speiser, E. A. *Oriental and Biblical Studies.* Philadelphia, 1967.

Spiegel, Shalom. "A Prophetic Attestation of the Decalogue." HTR 27 1934, pp. 120ff.

Stein, S. "The Dietary Laws in Rabbinic and Patristic Literature." *Studia Patristica* II, ed. by K. Aland and F. Cross. Berlin, 1957, pp. 141-154.

Stern, Herold S. "The Ethics of the Clean and Unclean." Judaism VI 1957, pp. 319-327.

Thompson, Stith. *Motif-Index of Folk-Literature.* Bloomington, 1933.

Tylor, E. B. *Researches in the Early History of Mankind,* ed. Paul Bohannan, Chicago, 1964.

van der Leeuw, G. *Religion in Essence and Manifestation.* New York, 1938.

————. Sacred and Profane Beauty. New York, 1963.

van Duhn, F. "Rot und Tot," *Archiv für Religionswissenschaft,* IX 1906, pp. 124ff.

van Gennep, Arnold. *The Rites of Passage.* Chicago, 1960.

von Rad, Gerhard. *Old Testament Theology.* London, 1963.

Vriezen, Th. C. *An Outline of Old Testament Theology.* Oxford, 1958.

Wachter, L. *Der Tod im Alten Testament.* Stuttgart, 1964.

Wagner, Geoffrey. *On the Wisdom of Words.* Princeton, 1968.

Wensinck, A. J. *Some Semitic Rites of Mourning and Religion.* Amsterdam, 1917.

Wevers, J. W. "Form Criticism of Individual Complaint Psalms." VT 6, 1956, pp. 82-83.

Wilson, John A. "Funeral Services in the Egyptian Old Kingdom." JNES 3 1944, pp. 203-204.

Wolff, H. W. *Amos' Geistige Heimat*. Neukirchen, Netherlands, 1964.

Zandee, J. *Death as an Enemy According to Ancient Egyptian Conceptions*. Leiden, 1960.

HEBREW WORKS CITED

Allon, Gedalyahu. *Meḥqarim Betoldot Yisrael*. Tel Aviv, 1970.

Alshikh, R. Moshe. *Commentary on the Book of Ruth*.

Braude, William G., transl. *The Midrash on Psalms*. New Haven, 1959.

————, transl. *Pesikta Rabbati*. New Haven, 1968.

Buber, Solomon, ed. *Midrash Agadah*. Reprinted Jerusalem, 1961.

————, ed. *Midrash Tanḥuma*. New York, 1946.

Chavel, C. P., ed. *Kitvei Rabbenu Baḥya*. Jerusalem, 1969.

————, transl. Maimonides, *The Commandments*. London, 1967.

————, ed. *Naḥmanides*. Jerusalem, 1965.

Denburg, C., transl. *Code of Hebrew Law: Yoreh De'ah*. Montreal, 1954.

Epstein, R. B. H. *Torah Temimah*. New York, 1928.

Goldin, Judah, transl. *The Fathers According to Rabbi Nathan*. New Haven, 1955.

Gross, M. D., ed. *Oẓar Ha-Aggadah*. Jerusalem, 1954.

Ha-Cohen, R. Yisrael Meir., ed. *Sifra*. Reprinted Jerusalem, 1969-70.

Ha-Levi, R. Aharon. *Sepher Ha-Ḥinukh*. Reprinted New York, 1962.

Heinemann, Y. *Ta'ame Hamitzvoth*. Jerusalem, 1963.

Herzog, R. Isaac Ha-levi. "On the Law of Burying an Apostate." *No'am*. Jerusalem, 1959, II, pp. 1-13.

Hutner, R. Isaac. *Paḥad Yitzḥak*. New York, 1950.

Hoffman, D. *VaYiqra*. Jerusalem, 1953.

Jellinek, A. *Bet Hamidrash*. Jerusalem, 1967.

Kaplan, Zvi. *Behalakhah Ve-'Agadah*. Jerusalem, 1959.

Kariv, A., ed. *Kithve Maharal Mi-Prague*. Jerusalem, 1960.

Lubavitch, R. Menaḥem Mendel of. *Derekh Mitzvosekha*. New York, 1953.

Peli, Pinchas, ed. *Al Hateshuva, Addresses of R. J. B. Soloveitchik*. New York, 1974.

Pines, S., ed. and transl. Maimonides, *The Guide of the Perplexed*. Chicago, 1963.

Rikanati, R. Menaḥem *Commentary on Bible*. Lublin, 1595.

Sabba, Abraham. *Tzeror Hamor*. Venice, c. 1576.
Samuel of Sokhotsov. *Shem Mishmuel*. Jerusalem, 1952 edition.
Sh'iltot of R. Aḥai Gaon. Jerusalem, 1961.
Sperling, A. I. *Taamei Ha-Minhagim*. Jerusalem, 1967.
Urbach, E. E. *Ḥazal*. Jerusalem, 1969.
Zlotnick, D., ed. *The Tractate Mourning*. New Haven: Yale Judaica Series, 1966.

Indexes

BIBLICAL

BABYLONIAN TALMUD
(in alphabetical order of Tractates)

(N.B.: The numerous references to Midrashim are in the footnotes and are not indexed.)

Baba Bathra	16a	83	Niddah	9a	67
Baba Bathra	91 a-b	113			
Baba Mezia	86a	115, 132	Qiddushin	23b	57
Berakhot	18a	76, 107			
Berakhot	18b	19	Sanhedrin	11a	110, 125
Berakhot	21b-22a	36	Sanhedrin	21b	xvi
Berakhot	33a	28	Sanhedrin	47b	69
Berakhot	51a	136	Sanhedrin	65a	22
Berakhot	59a	74	Sanhedrin	68a	111
Berakhot	66	111, 125	Sanhedrin	83a	59
'Erubin	54b	29	Semahot	1:9	116
			Semahot	6:3	100
Ketubot	17a	101	Semahot	8:7	132
Ketubot	46b	133	Semahot	11:4	116
Ketubot	104a	111, 124			
			Shabbat	30a	18, 107
Megillah	31b	29	Shabbat	105b	132
Megillah	6a	115, 116	Shabbat	106a	96
			Shabbat	152a	27, 94
Moed Qatan	14b	103, 104	Shabbat	152b	74
Moed Qatan	15a	86, 103			
Moed Qatan	15b	85, 95	Sotah	48b	125
Moed Qatan	17a	105			
Moed Qatan	19b	87	Temurah	32a	73
Moed Qatan	21a	100	Temurah	32b	73
Moed Qatan	23b	88			
Moed Qatan	25b	109, 113, 114, 117, 118, 129, 131	Yebamot	121b	115
			Yebamot	105b	29
Moed Qatan	27b	137	Yoma	39a	75
Moed Qatan	28b	112, 137	Yoma	67b	44

JERUSALEM TALMUD

Berakhot	2:7	85	Moed Qatan	3:5	88, 95, 100
Ketubot	1:1	80, 100			

MISHNAH

'Abot	3:3	26, 45	Negaim	3:1		65
'Abot	4:23	122	Negaim	12:1		65
			Negaim	11:1		65
Berakhot	5:2; 9:2	28				
Berakhot	3:3	37	Oholot	1:2		14
Kelim	2:1	14	Rosh Hashanah	4:5		28
Kelim	1:5-6	65				
Kelim	1:6-9	68	Sanhedrin	6:2		70
			Succah	5:1		134
Middot	2:2	105				
			Yadayim	3:5		66
Moed Qatan	3:8, 9	137	Yadayim	4:6		64
Negaim	12:1	65	Yoma	8:8		70

TOSEFTA

Yadayim	2:13	66	Yoma	4:9	70

SUBJECT INDEX